STRANGE DESTINIES

From the files and private records of one of the best-known authorities on psychic phenomena come these true, authenticated, classic tales of the inexplicable—stories that challenge the rules of science and the laws of nature—told as only a professional newspaperman-commentator can tell them.

Most of these extraordinary stories are published here for the first time, the details having been unavailable or deliberately suppressed until now. From the furthest reaches of the earth John Macklin has gathered his facts, to present a book you will find difficult to forget.

STRANGE DESTINIES

TRUE, documented accounts of unusual men and women, and spine-chilling journeys into time and space!

STRANGE DESTINIES

by

JOHN MACKLIN

ACE BOOKS, INC.
1120 Avenue of the Americas
New York, N.Y. 10036

An *ACE STAR* Book by arrangement with the author.

Printed in the U.S.A.

Table of Contents

THE MAN WHO WAS IN TWO PLACES AT ONCE

Was it a hoax or an uncanny gift?

As Roger sat in a guarded room, investigators phoned to say his manifestation was walking the streets of a distant city. And when eventually the "double" came on the telephone to repeat a secret password, it was the climax of the most remarkable case in psychic history.

WHEN DR. MARTIN SPENCER first heard about the man who could be in two places at once, it struck him as ideal material for a dinner party anecdote, but hardly worthy of serious investigation.

As director of Australia's Victoria Institute for Psychic Research he heard many stories of this kind but only perhaps one in a hundred was worthy of a researcher's time.

Over the years Dr. Spencer had developed an instinct for smelling out frauds, for catching out those people who got a kick out of fooling psychic researchers. And the case of the man in two places at once came, he decided, into this category.

For once he was wrong. In the spring of 1937 the apparently incredible ability of Louis Rodgers to appear simultaneously in places 500 miles apart burst into world headlines.

Scientists, researchers into the supernatural, doctors, even the police, subjected Louis Rodgers to unprecedented scrutiny. They followed him, traced his every contact, even locked him up.

Air of mystery

Yet as he sat in a guarded room in Melbourne investigators would be telephoning to report that his manifestation was walking the streets of distant Sydney.

The experts were baffled then, and they are today. If it was a hoax it was certainly the most skilled in the history of psychic investigation.

Louis Rodgers had come to Australia from England in 1931 as a man of thirty and set up in Melbourne as a medium and clairvoyant. Personable and handsome, he soon established a fairly lucrative practice among old ladies who wanted their loved ones brought back to them, an afternoon a week, at a reasonable price.

This Rodgers seemed able to do without much trouble. No one knew much about him. He had an air of mystery, and he cultivated it.

Rumors started

"I am at the mercy of the spirits," was his favorite phrase. "Wherever they summon me I must go." Most people regarded this as professional jargon, until one day in the summer of 1935 when two of Rodgers' clients met in a Melbourne street.

"I didn't know Mr. Rodgers had moved to Sydney," said one. "But my sister saw him there last Thursday afternoon and had quite a long conversation."

"That's impossible," said the other woman. "He was at my house last Thursday afternoon. He brought back my poor dead husband."

And so the rumors started. The spaces in Rodgers' appointment book became few and far between. The man of mystery became a living symbol of the existence of other worlds.

And whenever his clients could bring themselves to ask him about the rumors, Rodgers would smoothe back his long black hair and smile, his sad, enigmatic smile.

Angry refusal

The instances of his "double appearances" became numerous. Witnesses invariably found that if the Rodgers they were talking to was vigorous and animated, the "double" would be aloof and distracted.

Eventually the stories became so regular, so insistent, that scientists from Dr. Spencer's Institute asked Rodgers if he would submit to tests. Angrily he refused.

His refusal intrigued Spencer. He visited Rodgers in his drapery-hung consulting rooms and asked the medium what he feared.

Rodgers replied that his clients respected and trusted him and he had no intention of allowing mere scientific theorizing to jeopardize his career.

Eventually Dr. Spencer's persuasiveness won. With a final show of reluctance, Rodgers agreed to take part in a series of experiments.

But already official notice was being taken of his alleged powers. The police, anxious to know whether some type of confidence trick was being operated, were carrying out their own investigation into Rodgers' movements.

"He's here!"

Dr. Spencer's tests began in April, 1937. Rodgers agreed not to leave Melbourne for three weeks, and allowed researchers to "tail" him on all jaunts from his house.

On April 8, three days after the tests started, an investigator in Sydney reported that a man named Louis Rodgers had checked into a down-town hotel. He visited the hotel and knocked on the appropriate door. It was opened by a tall handsome man with long black hair. "Yes, I am Louis Rodgers," he said. "I have just come from Melbourne."

Bewilderedly, the investigator rang Spencer. "He's here," he babbled into the phone. "No, he isn't," said Spencer. "I'm having lunch with him at this moment."

Spencer was not overawed by the information. He realized that two smart operators looking reasonably alike, could easily pull off this trick. He told Rodgers so.

"I'm getting rather weary of all this," the medium replied. "On April 12 I will prove once and for all I have this extraordinary power. Then perhaps you'll leave me alone."

Tension mounted

So on Saturday, April 12, Rodgers was taken to Dr. Spencer's office and locked in. In the presence of three witnesses he asked Spencer for a password—the first word that came into his mind.

Spencer immediately said: "Lilac." The man sat there for an hour. Then the phone rang. It was a representative in Sydney reporting that he had seen, in a crowded street, a man who looked like Louis Rodgers.

Tension mounted in the room. Rodgers stared unconcernedly from the window.

At 5 P.M., an hour after the last call, the telephone rang

again. Spencer grasped the instrument, and switched on a monitoring tape recorder. "This is Sydney," said the operator. "I have a call for you."

Over the crackling wires came an unmistakable voice: "This is Louis Rodgers. The code word is Lilac. . . ."

Rodgers died in 1942, serving with the Australian Army in Europe. And the secret which died with him was either a hoax of breathtaking skill—or the most uncanny phenomenon yet known to man.

ROULETTE WHEEL OBEYED THE GAMBLER'S THOUGHTS!

His mind was master of the law of chance . . .

At Europe's elegant gaming tables, John Robertson made gambling history of a new and uncanny kind. There seemed no doubt, he had the power of mind over matter, and mastery of the spinning roulette ball. His gift brought him wealth, fame, and eventually complete and terrible ruin.

JOHN ROBERTSON was a poor man, but he had an uncanny gift. He was not a sparkling personality, but his brain had a potential which millionaires would have given fortunes to possess.

It took John Robertson some years to fully realize what power lay inside him. When he did, he exploited it to the full. It brought him wealth, and if not fame, certainly notoriety. But in the end, at the final reckoning, it brought him ruin.

For Robertson had the power of mind over matter. He could throw up a coin and make heads or tails come up according to his whim. He could decide in advance how dice would tumble.

In 1925, when he fully realized what mental power he had, Robertson set out to beat the gambling world at its own game—the game of roulette.

His performances at the tables of Deauville, Cannes, and finally Monte Carlo made gaming history of a new and uncanny kind.

His obsession

Five years earlier, John Robertson, at 34 a shiftless man of all trades, had landed in Britain from Australia.

In London he lived the aimless life of the casual laborer. With little money and no friends, he spent most of his evenings alone in a succession of dreary furnished rooms.

It was in one of these, in 1922, that he realized he had the power over dice. He had been playing idly with a set, vaguely thinking of numbers. Suddenly the realization hit him with a jolt: the numbers he thought of were the ones which appeared.

Soon the forecasting of numbers and circumstances became his hobby and then his obsession.

He experimented with spinning coins, with numbers of matches tipped out of a box, with the sequences of colored counters, and finally with a toy roulette wheel belonging to a neighbor.

His power

So it was that in 1925 John Robertson pawned and sold whatever he could lay his hands on, bought a couple of suits and some respectable-looking luggage and took a single ticket across the Channel to seek his fortune.

The gift Robertson possessed is now known to researchers

as "particular psychokinesis"—or P.K., a strange and unaccountable power which lies within the minds of a select few.

There is no scientific explanation—it just happens, perhaps once in a generation.

During the first few months of the season of 1925, Robertson visited the casinos of Paris, Nice, Deauville, and finally the white domed gambling palace of Monte Carlo.

He didn't play, only watched; estimating which game was most suited to the exploitation of his gifts.

Reluctantly he discarded the card games. Chemin-de-fer and particularly baccarat, offered glittering rewards—but he could not influence the run of cards.

.

The first time

All his mind could control was moving things . . . like the tiny ball which raced round the spinning roulette wheel. So roulette it was to be.

On August 4, 1925, Robertson took his place for the first time at the roulette table of Deauville's most exclusive casino, £100 worth of chips before him.

It was early evening, and few people were leaning against the brass rails behind the table, watching play.

Robertson started cautiously. He shut the elegance and bustle of the casino from his mind. Elbows on the green baize, he concentrated all his mental powers on the tiny ivory ball skidding on the merry-go-round of swirling numbers, willing it to fall in the slot he had backed.

The first time he lost. The second game, the ball hovered over his slot and slithered away. He concentrated more fiercely: suddenly the ball became his willing servant.

Couldn't lose

At the end of the evening he took an impressive pile of

13

chips over to the cashier's grille and exchanged them for
£500 worth of francs.

John Robertson, gambler, was in business.

The next few months read like a fairy tale. With a working
balance of £40,000, a silver-gray limousine, and a retinue of
hangers-on, Robertson toured the gambling centers. Seemingly he could not lose.

Late autumn found him at the tables of Monte Carlo's
Metropolitan Club. His gifts had become legend. Players at
other tables would see what he had backed and hurry to their
own games to lay identical bets.

After two nights, when he was £100,000 in credit, a man
approached the manager of the Casino and asked if he
would like Robertson's run of luck to be ended. His name,
he said, was Jean Leone, and he too had the gift of P.K.

"I haven't his uncanny skill," said Leone, "but I can at
least cancel out his thought-wave advantage." Eventually the
manager agreed. On the evening of September 30, Leone
lounged on the brass rails behind the players, watching
Robertson and particularly what numbers he backed.

Never again

Robertson was in his usual position, leaning forward, his
half-closed eyes fixed intently on the ball. He pushed forward £1,000 of chips on to number 14 on the board.

The game began. The ball skirted the wheel and rattled
into number three slot. The watchers stirred. Robertson lit
a cigarette and flicked more chips on to the board.

Again the white blob whirled on the moving red and black
circle. Again he lost, and again. Soon the crowd round the
table had swelled. Players left other tables—the impossible
had happened. Robertson was going down. Impassively Leone stood watching the game.

At 2 A.M. Robertson made his final fling. Every chip he
had went on number seven. The wheel spun. There was a

gasp. The croupier pushed forward his rake to claw away the chips. Robertson pushed back his chair and left the table, as penniless as that first day he entered a casino.

He never played again. He died in 1944 in a pauper's hospital in Belgium. There have been other epic gambling stories but surely none so strange as that of John Robertson who mastered that willing servant of chance, the ivory roulette ball.

THE NIGHT THE DEVIL STALKED THE STREETS

No earthly creature left these hoofmarks in the snow . . .

For over 100 miles the hoofmarks ran in an unbroken line. The creature that left them had scampered up walls and over rooftops, pranced along walls and fences. And it's journey had taken less that five hours. To hundreds of Dutch villagers it could only mean the Devil had roamed their streets. . . .

THE PEOPLE OF the Dutch fishing village of Scheveningen crowded into their church on the morning of January 9, 1913, to seek deliverance from the Devil.

Services in the village were usually well attended, for this was a pious Protestant community. But this day things were different. First, it was a Wednesday; and, second, the previous night the Devil had roamed their streets.

It could only have been he. His cloven hoofmarks were everywhere in the crisp, new snow which had fallen during the night.

He had scampered and pranced and slithered over fences and fields, over walls and rooftops, leaving thousands of hoofprints in an unbroken line to mark his passing.

What else could it have been, this thing which could travel up walls and over the rooftops of decent God-fearing folk? Where did it come from; where did it go?

Over the roof

Early on that cold morning, Wilhelm Crommelin, the village baker, had found the tracks as he unlocked his shop to start the daily baking. They came up the village street to his door. Then, about three feet away, they turned abruptly and vanished—just stopped short in the snow.

Crommelin walked out into the street, and glanced up to his roof. Unbelievably, the tracks went over his roof, down the other side, across his garden and out of sight.

He examined the tracks. They were made by a biped—but certainly not a human. The marks indicated a cloven hoof about the size of a small cow's.

In other communities in the district that morning, more people were making the same sort of discovery. Something had crossed the countryside at night, evidently after the snowfall had ceased, leaving a single line of tracks in the snow.

Villagers armed

They followed a course more than one hundred miles long, eventually ending near the water's edge to reappear several miles further along the coast. Whatever it was seemed equally at home on land or sea.

But what was it? By mid-morning the countryside was aroused and excited. Groups of men from the cluster of villages armed themselves with anything handy and went out to find what had by now been called "the monster."

Under a heading, "Extraordinary Circumstances," a newspaper carried a guarded report of the incident:

"The track appeared more like that of a biped than a quadruped, and the steps were generally two feet in advance of each other. The impression of the feet closely resembled a cow's hoof and measured about three inches across."

It was noted that the creature had approached the doors of many homes and retreated without giving any indication that it had paused to rest. Was it looking for something? If so, what?

Intriguing facet

Eight days after the incident there was still so much excitement about the matter that people were afraid to leave their homes at night unless in armed groups.

Efforts were made to track the starting point of the trail. Through fields and forests, hamlets and towns it went, over dykes—and out to the sea. Oddly, they ran in a straight line, one exactly before the other, mile after mile—to add another intriguing facet to the mystery. For no biped, apart from some species of bird, sets its feet down in ruler-straight lines.

Inevitably, experts appeared with explanations. One priest blandly assured his nervous parishioners that the footprints had been made by nothing more mysterious than a kangaroo! But all the solutions had one basic failing: they did not meet the circumstances.

Relentless speed

The thing had crossed large areas of very cold water, it had gone under low bushes without knocking snow from them, leaped easily from earth to rooftop, walked along walls and fences.

And, most baffling of all, it had done all these things at

relentless speed—for it was less than five hours between the time the snowfall stopped and the baker's discovery of the prints—not long for something on foot to cover well over 100 miles. . . .

Several thousand people saw the footprints before the weather obliterated them. No one could supply any theory which was even slightly plausible—except that they were the hoofprints of the Devil.

Eventually, research was able to throw a little light on the mystery—but get no nearer a solution. Years before, the Antarctic explorer, Captain James Ross, had come across a similar phenomenon.

Landing on a barren island called Kerguelen, on the fringes of the Antarctic, he wrote: "Of land animals we saw none, and the only traces we could discover were the singular footprints of a two-legged being with the hooves of a pony or ass.

Would it return?

"We traced these footprints for some distance in the recently-fallen snow in hopes of getting some sight of this strange creature, but we lost the tracks near the water's edge and presume they went into the sea."

Whatever it was, the Kerguelen creature resembled the Dutch one in two important respects: it made similar tracks and came out of—and disappeared into—the sea.

But to the people of Scheveningen and the surrounding villagers, Ross's observation only deepened their conviction that the thing that had come silently among them that snowy night was no earthly creature.

Would it come back?

But it didn't. Gradually, the excitement died down and the puzzling footprints ceased to be the major topic of conversation. Such things had never been seen before in Holland and have never been seen since.

There are people alive today who remember that January night. And most of them are convinced that, despite any scientific theory which might be advanced, it was the night when the Devil stalked the streets.

THE MAN WHO COULD FLOAT IN MID-AIR

And proved it 70 feet above the street . . .

Before witnesses and in broad daylight a man floated out of a 70 foot high hotel window, and lay there suspended in mid-air. No one has ever solved the mystery of this classic feat of levitation.

THE "extraordinary series of experiments conducted in cooperation with Mr. Daniel Dunglas Home," occupied well over half the column space in the summer edition of the *Quarterly Journal of Science.*

Finally, in large black type, came the august journal's verdict: "In our view there is no doubt that by some means outside our experience, Mr. Home is able to lift himself off the ground and propel himself considerable distances through the air."

The Journal of Science was only echoing what dozens of people had known for years—that Daniel Dunglas Home was a superman. But at last his activities had been given scientific assessment.

Not that Home needed the Journal's approval. In the closing years of the last century this Scottish-born mystic and spiritualist was a world celebrity.

Before witnesses, in broad daylight, he repeatedly performed spectacular feats of levitation which have never been surpassed. No one could explain his uncanny powers. And if he was a fraud, no one could catch him out.

Weird sounds

Daniel Home was born in Scotland and brought up in America. As a boy, he mystified and disturbed his parents by speaking to, and describing, things they could not see.

Soon he was known as the "boy wizard" and his tricks included making objects rise from tables and the production of weird knocking sounds from various corners of the room. But he was still regarded as little more than a conjurer and at the age of 25, went to Europe hoping that there his powers would be considered more seriously.

They were: soon Home was a celebrity. The fashionable and famous flocked to his seances. Never were they disappointed—the tall blue-eyed Scotsman always had something spectacular to show them.

Scientists restive

The rooms were always brightly lit—Home despised mediums who felt it necessary to work in shrouded gloom.

The poet Robert Browning attended a session during which a table rose three feet from the ground and traveled several yards across the room.

Many people believed such feats could only be performed by a man in league with the Devil—and this was given official confirmation when Rome ordered his expulsion from the Catholic Church for his "unseemly traffic with ghosts."

This publicity only added to Home's popularity. At informal seances in fashionable London homes, he would happily perform such tricks as playing the guitar without touching the instrument, or signing autographs when standing several yards away from the pen and paper.

But several eminent scientists and physiologists were getting restive.

"Veiled spirit"

It was time, they considered, that Home should submit his fantastic claims to expert adjudication. It was one thing to bewitch some bejewelled dowager; quite another to convince a hard-headed scientist.

To their surprise, Home agreed. His wife had recently died and now seances were further enlivened by the appearance of a "veiled female spirit."

Before the tests could be arranged, Home went off on an extended continental tour. Its highlights were seances given before the Queen of Holland, the King of Prussia and the Czar of Russia—and an unsuccessful attempt on his life by an assassin in Belgium.

On his return to Britain, he found that a suite in a London hotel had been booked and an exhaustive series of tests organized under the supervision of Sir William Crookes, a noted physicist and chemist.

Observers would include the Earl of Dunraven and Lord Brougham. All the tests would take place in broad daylight. Home agreed to all these conditions.

In a trance

On the first day, Home confined himself to handling fire with his bare hands, and ordering pieces of furniture to rise from the floor. The investigators moved around searching for hidden devices. They found nothing.

On the second day, reported Sir William in the *Quarterly Journal of Science,* "on three separate occasions I saw him raised completely from the floor of the room.

"He appeared in a trance. I passed my hands under his

feet and also touched the soles of his shoes. I could detect no apparatus or obstruction of any kind."

But it was on the afternoon of the second day that Home performed his feat which convinced Sir William and his colleagues that they were watching something not of this world.

Floated away

Deep in a trance, Home suddenly rose about five feet into the air and was transported horizontally across the room towards the open window.

Lord Dunraven ran across to prevent what surely would be disaster. But he was too late. Aghast the men watched, as Home floated out of the window and lay suspended, a few feet from the sill—and 70 feet above the street.

It was a fantastic sight. After a few seconds, the body began to rise, traveled past the window and into another one on the floor above. The men stood stunned. Then after a few seconds the door opened and Daniel Home came back into the room.

There was no need for any further tests. Shaken, the investigators left the hotel. "If a man had told me such a story," said Lord Dunraven, "I should have thought him either drunk or mad. But now I can believe that almost anything is possible."

Daniel Dunglas Home died at the age of 53. He had spent his life giving seances but he never made a penny out of his uncanny gifts.

WERE THESE CHILDREN FROM ANOTHER WORLD?

They came, hand in hand ... from a hole in the ground!

The mystery of the two green-skinned children is held up by psychic researchers as proof of a fourth dimension. Folklore, superstition, distortion, may have clouded the truth. But the fact remains: something inexplicable happened on that Spanish hillside one day in 1887.

ON AN AUGUST afternoon in 1887, two children walked hand-in-hand from a cave in a cliffside near the Spanish village of Banjos and into a field where farm workers were reaping.

It is nearly 80 years ago, but there are people alive who knew those who remembered the day.

There has been exaggeration undoubtedly, distortion too, but the basic facts seem to be indisputable: the children who walked fearfully from the cave spoke a strange and incoherent language, their clothes were of a substance never seen before.

And their skins were green.

It is a bizarre story containing no logic, no explanation. Yet psychic researchers pinpoint it as perhaps the most valuable evidence they have of the existence of a fourth dimension—a world existing side by side with ours, a twilight world from which the children had in some way escaped.

Priest's questions

The theory is that they had fallen into a space vortex—

like a man who falls through a hole in the ice and cannot rediscover the point of entry—had entered our third dimensional plane from a fourth, and could not get back.

Ridiculous? Possibly, but of all the theories put forward to account for the appearance of the green children, it is the only one which bears even a second glance.

Soon after the phenomenon, a priest came from Barcelona to investigate. He saw the children, questioned witnesses.

Later he wrote: "I was so overwhelmed by the weight of so many competent witnesses that I have been compelled to accept it as a matter I am unable to comprehend and unravel by the powers of intellect."

It was not surprising. The more evidence he collected, the less chance there seemed of any rational explanation.

Would not eat

The reapers were resting after lunch when the strange pair appeared in the entrance of a hillside cave. They were bewildered, weeping inconsolably—and their skins were a deep green.

Unbelieving, the workers hurried towards them. Frightened, the pair began to run. The excited men chased after them: the strange beings, babbling unintelligibly, were seized and borne to the village.

They were taken to the house of Ricardo da Calno, magistrate, and the village's chief landowner. While onlookers gaped through the windows, da Calno tried to speak to the pair.

He took the hand of the girl and rubbed it: the color stayed fast. It was undoubtedly part of the pigment of the skin. The child shrank away, crying with fear.

Food was placed in front of them, but they did not eat. They handled bread and fruit with a mixture of suspicion and wonder but would not put it near their mouths.

Only beans

He noted their features, though regular, were slightly negroid, the eyes almost almond shaped, and deep set.

The children stayed in the house for five days. They ate nothing and grew noticeably weaker. No food could be found which would tempt them.

Then one day, says a report, "beans cut or torn from stalks were brought into the house, and they fell on them with great avidity. But they broke open not the pod but the stalks, evidently supposing that the beans were in the hollows of the stalks.

"When finding nothing, they again began to weep. Then someone showed them how to open the pods. Whereupon, with great joyfulness, they ate many beans—and from then on would touch no other food."

But the fasting, it seems, had done serious harm to the boy. In spite of the beans, he grew weaker and finally died a month after being found. He was buried in the village graveyard.

"Always twilight"

The girl, however, grew stronger and became a servant in da Calno's house. Her green color faded somewhat and she became less of a curiosity in the village.

After a few months she had picked up a certain amount of Spanish and was able to give da Calno some sort of explanation of her arrival.

But if anything, it only deepened the mystery. She said she came from a land where no sun rises, and where it was always twilight. "Yet there is a land of light to be seen not far from us, but cut off by a stream of great width."

How had they arrived on earth? All she could say on this

was: "There was a great noise. We were caught up in the spirit and found ourselves in your harvest field."

That was all she said, and probably all she knew. She lived another five years before she too, died and is buried beside her brother.

A strange tale. Is it a garbled folk myth from the past, a hoax, a tall story gullibly passed from one generation to the next?

Ominous coincidences

The documents are still in existence: the sworn statements of witnesses who claimed to have spoken to, and touched, the beings who came hand-in-hand from a hole in the ground.

And there are theories, for instance, that they came from Mars—a cold planet where the flora may be blue or green, similar to that found in Alpine heights.

And scientists have long known that continual underground living brings on a bluish-green pallor.

Turning to the exotic legends of folk-lore, there are some strange and ominous coincidences. For instance, beans have for centuries been traditionally the food of the dead.

And even today, among American Indians there are myths and legends about a subterranean world in which civilized men are forced to dwell, after a collision of the North Pole with a tremendous thunderbolt had sunk a continent.

None of these things sheds any light on the truth of the tale of the green children. But perhaps they make us a little more reluctant to condemn it as nonsense.

RIDDLE OF THE LIVING STONES

Could this man create creatures from the dust?

*Science experts fiercely denounced Andrew Crosse—
and his experiments. He claimed to have created insect
life in his laboratory . . . from porous stone, acid and an
electric charge! Even Crosse himself was mystified.
But the insects did exist—some even appeared under
the gaze of his critics.*

THE FARMERS and villagers who lived in and around the
sleepy English hamlet of Elworthy, nestling in Somerset's
Quantock Hills, regarded Andrew Crosse as more a devil than
a man.

They did not understand the livid flashes which lighted
his laboratory windows at night. They called him the "thunder and lightning man," and denounced him as an atheist and
blasphemer who should not be allowed to wander freely.

On the face of it, Andrew Crosse was a harmless little
chap. In middle age he had inherited a well-mortgaged and
poorly kept estate in the Quantocks, and settled down to
paying off his inherited debts and spending what spare time
he had in scientific research.

In the summer of 1900, Crosse conducted an experiment
in his ramshackle laboratory which set the scientific world
quivering with a mixture of ridicule and incredulity . . .

He had, he claimed, discovered the "spark of life"—an
electric flash which transformed a chunk of stone into a mass
of living, moving creatures. It was either a miracle or a
fraud, and to this day scientists do not know which.

Mystery force

How could an electric explosion endow stone with life and breath, movement and instinct? Even Crosse could not explain his discovery.

"I have never never ventured an opinion on the cause of the phenomenon," he explained in a paper to the London Electrical Society, "for a very good reason—I was never able to form one."

Was some mystery force released by the chance meeting of electricity and stone? Had Crosse stumbled accidentally on some key to creation; eavesdropped on some fourth dimensional process normally hidden from human sight?

Throughout his life, Crosse labored under the double handicap of not understanding his own experiments and not knowing about the accomplishments of others.

But it was perhaps this very lack of knowledge which led to the experience which has become a scientific classic.

Neighbors alarmed

Pottering round his laboratory, one day, he decided to conduct experiments on the formation and development of artificial crystals by means of exposure to electric currents.

He rigged up a piece of porous stone, kept it electrified by means of a crude battery, and submerged the whole apparatus in a trough of acid.

Crosse set the equipment on a small table and went back to his regular pastime of studying the spark gap—so causing the flashes which alarmed his neighbors.

From time to time he had a look at the stone in the acid, but nothing appeared to be happening. He took the stone from the acid and placed it on a dish where it crumbled into a mixture of ash and dust.

On the fourteenth day, Crosse peered through a lens at the dish and noted whitish, pointed bumps protruding from it.

Died in a week

Every day they grew longer, and by the 28th day Crosse wrote excitedly in his notebook: "These appearances have assumed the form of a *perfect insect* standing erect on a few bristles which form its tail.

"Until this period I had no notion that these appearances were anything but mineral formations. On the thirtieth day these creatures moved their legs.

"I must say that I was not a little astonished. After a few days they detached themselves from the dust and moved about at pleasure."

In the course of a few weeks, about a hundred of the creatures made their appearance in the dish. He examined them with a microscope and observed that the small ones had six legs, and the larger eight legs. They did not appear to be of any recognized species.

Within a week they died, and Crosse set about creating some more. He was well aware of the tightrope he was walking. He was experiencing something which did not fit into the accepted pattern of science.

Denounced as fraud

He suspected the insects might be stowaways in the porous stone, so he dispensed with stone entirely and conducted experiments with oxide powder and acids. Once again the creatures appeared.

By now he had been denounced as a fraud. Learned men condemned both Crosse and his insects as humbugs. The creatures, they said, were nothing more than the products of airborne spores or of impurities in the fluids themselves.

Anticipating this, Crosse had already begun a new series of experiments designed to determine whether the things he saw were the result of simple electrical generation and nothing more. He boiled his jars, baked his apparatus, sterilized all his materials. Yet 140 days after he sent electric current into his sealed air-free jars, the creatures appeared as before.

By now scientists began to appear in the Quantocks. Crosse was pleased to let them see his experiments.

Standing alone

They watched as dust came to life. They couldn't explain the phenomenon—but they called Crosse a fraud all the same.

As more people went to see for themselves the mystifying developments in his laboratory, Crosse became the center of a major scientific row. Standing virtually alone against a tide of calumny, he could only repeat doggedly that he had told the truth, as some of his detractors could readily determine if they conducted similar experiments.

"I have merely tried to report what I have seen and the conditions under which these things have transpired," he explained. "Sometimes I wish I had kept silent about them."

Science progressed, and Crosse was soon forgotten. In 1903 he died in a fire which burned his laboratory and all his samples.

Born in fire, they were destroyed by it—and with them died all chance of solving the baffling mystery of how life was created by a flash of light.

HAUNTED BY THE GHOST OF A MAN STILL ALIVE!

—and it saved his life 10 years later . . .

Lord Dufferin would never forget the face of the man who carried a coffin across a moonlit lawn. It was baleful and unbelievably evil. Ten years later he saw it again—on a living man. And the sight of it saved Dufferin from a terrible and violent death.

THE FOYER of Paris' Grand Hotel was brimming with diplomats and embassy staff. They crowded round the lifts waiting to be taken up to the banqueting hall where the first—and largest—diplomatic reception of the 1898 season was to be held.

One of the ornate wrought-iron lifts was being reserved for V.I.P.s. A commissionaire shouldered back the throng as a line of ambassadors and equerries trooped in.

Eventually the First Marquess of Dufferin and Ava, British Ambassador to Paris, came to the entrance of the lift.

Officials stood back respectfully as he passed. Then he stopped. He went pale. He put out his hands and stopped his secretary from entering.

He turned away from the lift, white and shaking, and a buzz of consternation arose. The doors clashed shut and the lift rose, taking twelve men to their doom.

Never forgot

Lord Dufferin was saved from sharing their fate by the

31

sight of a face the memory of which had haunted him for ten years.

It was baleful, contorted and unbelievably malicious. And Lord Dufferin had last seen those features on the face of a ghost.

Lord Dufferin was a distinguished man. He had been Governor General of Canada, Viceroy of India and Ambassador to Rome and Moscow.

He had always professed a profound disbelief in the supernatural—at least until the summer of 1878 when he had his first sight of the face which he never again forgot.

That summer he accepted an invitation from a friend to stay in Ireland. On June 14, Lord Dufferin went to bed, but found himself unable to sleep.

At midnight he dozed off, and awoke suddenly to find the room's atmosphere had strangely changed. It seemed charged with something electric.

The moonlight fell on to the lawns outside his window and brought into relief the dark bushes beyond. Through the whispering of the wind he heard a long low moaning.

He left his bed and went to the window. He opened a french door leading on to a terrace and looked out into the gardens. The sounds appeared to come from the shadows cast by a bank of trees.

Dufferin stood peering into the shadows when suddenly something began to move. The moaning and panting continued. Then, as he watched, a figure came out of the dark into the full light of the moon.

It was a man, staggering under the weight of an enormous coffin. Body-snatching was not unknown. Dufferin, still convinced he was dealing with a human, hurried across the lawn shouting: "Look here! What have you got there?"

No footprints

At this challenge, the man lifted his head from under his

burden. The face Dufferin saw was of such ghoulish ugliness, so terribly repulsive, that he fell back a step. The contorted vileness burned itself indelibly on his mind.

Nerving himself he called again: "Where are you taking that?" and stepped towards the man. Incredibly, both man and coffin vanished.

There were no footprints on the dewy grass. Nothing but the mocking moonlight and the eerie noises of the night.

Dufferin returned to his room. There he wrote down every detail of the strange occurrences in his diary.

After breakfast, he questioned his host. But he found there had been no death or recent burial in the village. Nor could anyone recognize his description of the man with the coffin.

Start of horror

There the mystery stood—for ten years. The incident became blurred in Dufferin's mind. All except the face. That stood out, hateful and razor sharp.

So the scene switched to Paris, and to the reception at the Grand Hotel.

The lift door was open and Dufferin was about to enter—when his eye fell on the attendant. He recoiled with a start of horror. There was the face . . .

There was the same ghoulish leer, the same contorted features, the same unforgettable squat body. Dufferin, with a supreme effort, kept himself under control.

He turned away, explaining that he felt ill. His secretary led him to a chair and the lift doors closed.

Ghastly accident

The lift car rose out of sight, and Dufferin got up and made for the manager's office.

He wanted desperately to know who the attendant was,

where he came from. But before the manager could answer, a terrible crash was heard.

Dufferin's secretary ran into the office with the news: there had been a ghastly accident. Already cries of anguish were confirming his story.

As the lift that Dufferin had refused to enter had risen to the fifth floor, the cables unaccountably broke. The lift had crashed down the shaft fatally injuring all who were inside it. Among the dead was the lift operator.

Who was he? No one ever knew. No one of that description could be found on the personnel lists.

But of one thing Lord Dufferin was sure: he had seen the lift operator's ghost 10 years before—while the man was still alive. . . .

HITLER BEGS FORGIVENESS FROM THE GRAVE!

—as voices of the dead return on tape . . .

In an artist's studio in Stockholm, an uncanny drama is being played out. A tape recorder is acting as a bridge between life and death—reproducing the voices of people long since dead. Hitler and Eva Braun have both been heard; so, too, have Bismarck and Napoleon.

IT WAS nearing lunchtime on April 4, 1960, when the clerks at the tape-recorder counter of Stockholm's largest electrical store were approached by a heavily-built, elderly man who hesitantly asked to see the manager.

It had taken 60-year-old Friedrich Jurgenson weeks to screw up enough courage to bring his tape-recorder back to the store where he had bought it.

He was an artist of some repute. A one-man exhibition of his work was opening at a city gallery the following week-end. He did not want to be labeled as a crank.

Jurgenson took his machine into the manager's office and placed it on the desk.

No, he had no complaints. The machine was working well. Nevertheless, he wanted a complete overhaul down to the last connection, the last nut and bolt, and would pay happily for the work.

Hurt and upset

"I will come back next week," he said, "to see if you have found anything irregular about the machine. You may think me eccentric, but you would undoubtedly think me mad if I told you now why I want the report."

The machine was found to be faultless. Matter-of-factly, Jurgenson told his story. Within hours it was in the newspapers: Friedrich Jurgenson's tape-recorder could pick up the voices of the dead.

Sceptics were quick to point out that such a device was tailormade for a hoax. Tapes could be faked or tampered with.

If Jurgenson had created the story as publicity for his exhibition, he surely could have thought of something a bit more original?

It seems strange that Jurgenson had not bargained for so much ridicule, but he hadn't. He was hurt and upset. He invited engineers, scientists, psychic researchers—anyone who wished—to examine the machine and hear the voices.

Cacophony of sound

It was in the early spring of 1960, that Jurgenson first discovered his tape-recorder was acting as a bridge between life and death.

He had no mechanical aptitude; in fact he boasted he could not mend a fuse, but he bought the tape-recorder to make notes for paintings as they occurred to him.

He set the machine up in his study on the outskirts of the city, ready for use. It stood idle for a week while Jurgenson worked on a still life for his exhibition.

On the Friday night he had some ideas about a portrait he was painting, switched on the machine and began to set down random thoughts.

But when he played it back, he was startled to hear a cacophony of sound interrupting his voice.

Coherent voices

Thinking the tape was at fault, he selected an unused one, ran it through the machine to ensure it was clean of recording, and re-recorded his notes. Again, the interruptions occurred.

This time, through a confusion of sound, coherent voices began to emerge. They set up an eerie chant which reverberated round his studio: "We live, we live. We are not dead." Then they faded. The tape rolled on, silent now.

Understandably, Jurgenson disbelieved his ears. He rewound the machine, played it again. The voices were still there, recorded indelibly on the tape.

On subsequent days, he used the machine frequently—and every time the mysterious interlopers interrupted his thoughts with plaintive exclamations.

He did everything he knew to rule out normal explanations for the phenomenon. He bought new tapes; he checked, as well as he could, the wiring and components of the recorder. Finding nothing, he took it back to the shop.

"This is Hitler!"

When the mystery became public, experts gathered regularly in his rooms. They searched his studio for hidden equipment, minutely examined his recorder and tapes, monitored the recording sessions. No trace of fraud could be detected.

Jurgenson went on recording. One day in August 1960 in the presence of ten witnesses he picked up a voice delivering a diatribe in a foreign language.

Suddenly a German technician sitting near the machine exclaimed: "That's Hitler!"

And so it was. Recordings in a radio station library matched perfectly with the voice on Jurgenson's tape. On it, the voice appeared to be addressing someone in a concentration camp.

It expressed regret for the atrocities committed during the last war.

No explanation

Few people laugh at Jurgenson now. Reporters visit him regularly to collect the latest sensation. Rarely does he disappoint them. Over the years, he collected 80 tapes containing almost 140 identifiable voices.

They include German statesman Bismarck, Napoleon, Lloyd George, and American murderer Caryl Chessman.

Jurgenson can offer no explanation for the phenomenon. Obviously, he says, his tape-recorder appears to have been selected as a go-between for the voices of the dead. But how, or why? He doesn't know.

The phenomenon continues. The latest name on the distinguished cast list is Hitler's mistress, Eva Braun, who has told, in a high-pitched whisper, about her wedding to the Fuhrer and their last hours together.

And in his studio, where now little painting is done, Friedrich Jurgenson sits by his recorder waiting for the next voices from the dead.

HAS THIS BOY LIVED BEFORE?

At five, he remembers the day he died!

Uncannily, vividly, little Edward Cabrero remembers a previous life on earth. He talks of the night he died. The mystery reached its bizarre climax the day he took his wondering parents to a strange town to meet his "other mother."

THEY TOOK little Edward Cabrero down the street of a strange town and he behaved as though he had come home. They confronted him with people he had never met, and he knew their names and greeted them as friends.

His parents wept as he went up to a middle-aged woman standing distraught in the street, and said happily: "This is my other mother."

For there seemed little doubt that the impossible had happened: that the personality of another child whom they never knew, and who is now dead, had taken over Edward Cabrero.

Today, Edward lives in the unclouded world of a five-year-old with his family in a suburb of Havana, Cuba. He talks repeatedly of his "other life," of the friends he made, the things he did. He talks of the night he died.

Experts have compiled detailed dossiers on the case, have tested the boy, tried to trick him. But Edward continues to supply information he could not possibly obtain in any orthodox way about a boy who died before he was born.

Dream life

At first they laughed when Edward, at three, began to tell stories about two brothers named Mercedes and Jean, and about a beautiful mother with fair skin and black hair.

"The boy is making up little stories," his parents told each other. "How charming," said their friends. "How clever of him."

It was a phase, no doubt, which he would grow out of. But as the months went by, Edward talked more and more about his "dream life."

His mother, he said, used to make hats. Sometimes she sent him on errands to nearby shops, particularly to a chemist whose goods were cheaper than elsewhere. But he preferred longer errands because then he could use the bicycle which was kept in a downstairs room.

First clue

The stories were so coherent, so consistent, that the family doctor, hearing one while making a call at the house, was intrigued. He sat the boy on his knee and questioned him gently.

Edward told him of how he had become very ill. His mother had cried a great deal, particularly when an ambulance came to take him to the hospital. But he never got to the hospital, for in the ambulance he had died.

"I remember the light coming through the windows gradually fading," said Edward. "I was tired but not frightened or unhappy."

"What was your name?" asked the doctor.

"Pancho Seco," said the boy. "We lived in the Rue Campanario, in Nuevitas." At least there was a definite clue. Edward's mother had relations in Nuevitas. She also knew that her son had never been there.

"There it is!"

One week-end, the Cabreros took Edward on an outing to Nuevitas. Rounding a corner, they faced a chemist's shop. "Look," cried the boy, "there it is—that's the shop I used to go to!"

He tugged his parents along the street and around another corner—into the Rue Campanario. He ran to number 69, shouting: "This is my house."

His father knocked, but there was no one in. Shaken, the family returned to Havana, where the local association of psychic research was consulted. Could this be a case of reincarnation?

How else could such a young child have accumulated such a wealth of detailed accurate information?

By now, Mrs. Seco had been contacted . . . at number 69, Rue Campanario. Yes, she said, their son Pancho had died four years ago.

A dossier

Would she take part in the experiment? Reluctantly, she agreed. Escorted by a team of researchers, little Edward returned to Nuevitas.

With them the researchers brought the dossier compiled from Edward's recollections of his previous life. His mother's first name was Amparo, his father's Pierro. He had two brothers.

Behind the house, he said, had run the railway. His father worked for the post office and rode to work on a blue bicycle. He named places in the country where the family had been taken on excursions and described in detail what had happened on these occasions.

He described a dog he had had, said its name was Tolo, described how it had been killed by a tram.

In all, the dossier contained 53 such details of routine family life. Unbelievingly, Mrs. Seco ticked them all as being accurate: most of them were things that only her son Pancho could have known.

Mother wept

Researchers persuaded Mrs. Seco to stand in a busy street, while Edward was taken past by his father. He spotted the woman immediately and shouted excitedly: "There's my other mother—over there by the shop window."

Mrs. Cabrero wept, and the other woman hurried away, unable to face the uncanny phenomenon.

In another test, the boy picked out Pancho's relatives and friends from a large crowd and addressed them by names which only Pancho had known and used.

Today, Edward still astounds and perturbs his parents by revealing new facts about his previous life. They live in an agony of doubt and bewilderment.

But month by month, as Edward's memories take shape, they are convinced that a dead child's spirit lives on in their son.

NIGHTMARE DRIVE—WITH NO ONE AT THE WHEEL

Police couldn't catch the car that drove itself . . .

A 30-mile stretch of road was the scene of a score of terrifying incidents as people fled from the path of a car which apparently had no one at the wheel. And what started as a routine case of theft became a classic mystery.

VINCENT MANSFELT, chief photographer of a Rotterdam evening newspaper, parked his car in the main square of the Dutch town of Eindhoven, took out the ignition key, turned a secret switch hidden under the dashboard and locked the doors.

All his actions were the routine gestures of the experienced motorist, but on the morning of September 13, 1934, they had a particular significance for Vincent Mansfelt. Later, he was to go over them again and again—with his employers, with the police and with himself.

For September 13 was the day his car drove itself away. Hours later, it was found 30 miles away in the town of Tilburg, still locked, the secret switch still turned off, no fingerprints on the steering wheel.

Yet the road between Eindhoven and Tilburg had been the scene of a score of terrifying incidents as people fled from the path of a car which apparently had no one at the wheel.

The story of Vincent Mansfelt's runaway car, at first suspected, later derided, has become a classic mystery.

No rush

Initially the case was regarded as a routine vehicle theft. Yet the more the police probed, the more confused the issues became.

Vincent Mansfelt's car was two years old and he spent most weekends tinkering with it and polishing its gleaming paintwork. He was proud of it; that was why he had had the anti-theft switch fitted.

On that Friday in September he had driven up to Eindhoven from Rotterdam to take pictures of the opening of a power station.

The photographs were not to appear until the next day. There was no rush to get back, so Mansfelt went to the official luncheon after the opening. It was not until nearly 3:30 P.M. that he made tracks for his car.

But his parking space in the square was empty.

Veered towards him

Mansfelt went to the police. He reported the theft and waited while initial inquiries were made. Had the car been officially moved for causing obstruction? Had the car park attendant ordered it to be shifted?

But the solution was not so simple. The car was marked down as missing presumed stolen, and Mansfelt despondently left the police headquarters and caught a train back to Rotterdam.

It could have been the end of the story. In fact, it was only the beginning.

At 2:30 P.M. roadworker Peter Crommelin was scything grass by the side of the southbound road a few miles outside Eindhoven, when he saw a black sedan of French manufacture, round a corner, veer over the middle line and slew straight towards him.

Instinctively, Crommelin threw himself to his left. The car lurched on to the grass verge, straightened, and sped away down the road. Shaken, Crommelin got to his feet and shouted after the car.

Ran for their lives

Then he noted a strange thing: there was nothing to obstruct his view through the back window to the windshield. He took the number of the car and telephoned the police from a nearby house.

A police patrol, alerted ten miles outside Tilburg, was waiting in a side road for the car. It came by at such a pace that by the time the police driver had pulled out, the stretch of main road was empty.

The police crew reported the same thing: either the driver was extremely small—or there was no one in the car.

In the next village a group of people crossing the road towards a bus stop ran for their lives as the car hurtled through. By the time the police patrol arrived, the car had disappeared.

A few miles away a herd of cows being driven along a minor road, stampeded in terror as a car drove through them without slackening speed. Again the drover reported: "I couldn't see anyone in the driving seat."

No one there

The police and the runaway car came face to face at last outside the hamlet of Visser. Police driver Hans Manders accelerated up to over 70 and came level with the runaway car, intending to force it into the grass verge.

As they hurtled along side by side the police observer craned over to peer into the driver's seat.

He later testified: "I am prepared to swear any oath that there was no one in the car."

Manders tried to edge the other vehicle off the road. Suddenly it veered across with a lurch, forcing the police car into the curb and grinding off its nearside rear tire.

The police car was able to stop without injury to the crew; the other vehicle drove away out of sight.

Terror drive

At 3:30 P.M. a policeman on patrol found Mansfelt's car parked at the curb near Tilburg town hall. It was dusty and the wings bore evidence of recent scraping.

When the car was eventually opened, the ignition was turned off, but the petrol tank was virtually empty.

A full inquiry was ordered. Mansfelt testified he had lent the car to no one; witnesses of the terror drive, including the police patrol, lamely explained how the car had appeared empty.

After acrimonious argument and testy protestations by the presiding magistrate that he was being asked to listen to fantasy, the inquiry was adjourned. It was never re-opened.

Vincent Mansfelt took his car and sold it to a scrap metal dealer. From that day until his death in 1950 he never drove a car again.

MURDERED ... BY HANDS OF STONE

Did phantom knights wreak cottage havoc?

Two stone effigies vanished from a tomb top. Later a young wife was found dead among the wreckage of her home. These two events were the vital clues in a horrific and classic mystery which has never been resolved.

ROBERT SANDFORD and his young wife Mary searched for several months before they found the cottage of their dreams. It was picturesque, a little ramshackle, and stood by a stream on the edge of a thick wood of yews.

In the spring of 1901, the Sandfords moved from London to their new home near Ashbourne, in England's lonely Peak District. The only other building in the vicinity was an old Norman church also half shrouded in the wood.

To this sylvan scene came a series of horrific incidents now firmly classified as classics of the unknown. Within a few months, Mary Sandford was dead—murdered while she sat alone in her cottage.

But no human committed the crime. The hands that choked the life from her body were made of . . . stone.

The cottage the Sandfords had made their home was built on the site of a former manor house which had belonged to two brothers who, according to local legend, were so lawless that it was only with difficulty that their relatives obtained for them Christian burial.

STRANGE DESTINIES

No doubt

They were interred in the yard of the Norman church, and over their bones was erected a tomb with effigies of their recumbent figures lying side by side on the marble slab.

The young couple were amused to hear that on All Soul's Day the stone effigies were reputed to leave their slabs and visit the scene of their old crimes—the spot on which the cottage now stood.

On an autumn day in 1901, shortly after tea, Robert Sandford decided to take a walk in the falling dusk. His wife, feeling tired, stayed by the fire.

Sandford strolled along a path which led through the churchyard. Suddenly he stopped and stood staring, almost doubting the evidence of his senses.

Through the trees, the tomb of the evil knights glowed whitely against the dark sky. Every detail was thrown into sharp relief. There was no doubt: the slab on the top of the tomb was unquestionably empty. The effigies had gone.

No joke

Instantly, he thought their disappearance must be the work of some practical joker, but he realized no man could lift the huge stone figures and carry them away.

In shocked perplexity he hurried towards his home, but on the way stopped, and retraced his steps. He couldn't believe what he had seen.

Entering the churchyard again, he walked boldly up to the tomb and thrust a lighted match towards the marble surface. There lay the figures, exactly as they had always been.

Striking countless matches, he examined every detail of the tomb. Nowhere was there a sign of any recent disturbance

—except that one figure had two fingers missing on the right hand, a small defect he presumed he had never noticed before.

At last, Sandford turned away, unaccountably relieved. He had suffered from some trick of light or perhaps a hallucination. He wondered whether to tell his wife. Would it frighten her, or would she only laugh at his story?

No sound

He made his way out of the churchyard and along the path leading back to the cottage. It was now almost dark. As he drew near, he gave a whistle which always heralded his approach, and which his wife invariably answered.

This time there was no answering sound. Nor was there any welcoming light in any of the windows. Sandford instinctively knew that something was terribly wrong.

He ran forward shouting her name. Tearing open the cottage door he was met by a strange, petrifying stillness.

He had used all his matches when investigating the tomb, and now he had to grope for others, still shouting his wife's name in ever-increasing alarm.

When he eventually found some and kindled a flame in a lamp, he could hardly believe what he saw.

The little sitting-room looked as though it had been wrecked by a bomb.

The stone floor was split as though it had been subjected to shattering blows, the walls were cracked and battered and a heavy table had been overturned and splintered.

On the floor, Sandford found the body of his wife. In the official police report of the tragedy, he recalled that her face "had an expression of such frozen horror which it was fearful to contemplate."

Mary Sandford had been strangled. Shattered and weeping, her young husband ran the three miles to the nearest village for help.

Soon police from Ashbourne joined with villagers to search for the assassin. No one was ever apprehended.

The last time

The day before the funeral, Robert Sandford sat in his cottage by the body of his dead wife.

He was thinking for the thousandth time of his experience in the churchyard, of the eerie legends of the All Soul's Day, and of the atmosphere of doom he had found when returning to the house.

What human force could have shattered the cottage in such a violent fashion? He looked at the pits gouged in the hard limestone floor, the deep fissures in the walls.

For the last time, he held his wife's frail hand. It was tightly clenched. Gently he straightened the fingers and a small piece of white stone clattered on to the floor.

Robert Sandford picked it up. On the stone were carved two marble fingers.

DEATHBED VOW: "I'LL KILL FROM THE GRAVE"

—and she murdered her nephew a year later . . .

"Yes, you will have my money," Marie Giscard told her nephew, "but spend it fast—for you will die within a year." And so he did, amid a horror of flailing hooves on a moonlit lawn—ridden down by a spectral horsewoman.

WHEN HE HEARD that Marie Giscard was dying, M. Paul Lecourt arranged for a flag to be flown from his house in

Paris' Rue de Somme, and ordered an oyster supper at the Cafe de la Paix.

The next day, in high spirits, he set off for La Rochelle, the town in the northwest of France where Marie Giscard was spending her last hours. He took with him a volume of Balzac to read on the journey and a suit of black for the funeral.

He knew he would return a rich man. For Marie Giscard, his aunt, had willed her fortune to him. Not surprisingly, Lecourt was Mme. Giscard's favorite relation. They had a lot in common: both were selfish, greedy and universally disliked.

On August 4, 1911, Lecourt reached the tiny chateau where his aunt was dying. She greeted him with cordial malevolence from her huge pink-draped four-poster. "Yes, you will have my money, Paul," she told him, "but spend it fast, because you will die within a year of me."

"And how do you know that, dear aunt?" he asked. "Because," she said, answering his mocking smile, "I will kill you myself."

Not worried

It was five days later that Paul Lecourt returned to Paris to arrange for £250,000—the proceeds of the sale of his aunt's estate—to be paid into his bank. He sold his house in the Rue de Somme and bought an apartment near the Champs Elysees. He was seen at every gala night, every fashionable reception; he escorted the city's most beautiful women.

If he remembered his aunt's deathbed curse he certainly gave no indication that it worried him.

In the spring of 1912, Paul Lecourt, now 35, became engaged to Edith Rochereau, 25-year-old daughter of the French Secretary of Housing. He had no illusions about being in love—but the engagement gave him an entree into government circles. He began to be seen at diplomatic events.

There was some talk of his being offered a Foreign Service post.

Only one thing had been salvaged by Lecourt from his aunt's former home. In his living room, a large portrait of Marie Giscard scowled down. It seemed to imprint its malice on the room. The corner in which it hung always seemed dark.

Fled in terror

One evening in May 1912, Edith Rochereau was waiting in the room while her fiancé dressed upstairs. They were going to the opera. Idly examining the pictures, the girl came to the portrait of Marie Giscard.

Suddenly as she lingered before it, the canvas became blurred, exhibiting a curious milky surface, and momentarily she seemed to visualize a room and a man in old-fashioned dress painting the portrait.

Then the vision faded and the face of Marie Giscard once again emerged—but now it was no portrait but a living fearsome woman with malignant, piercing eyes.

With a shriek of terror, the girl turned and fled from the room, sobbing and incoherent. Eventually, accompanied by Lecourt and a servant, she was persuaded to enter the room again—and the picture was quite normal.

"That is my aunt," Lecourt told her. "She promised to kill me before August." He seemed to treat the whole affair as a joke.

Thundering hooves

As summer approached, the fashionable citizens of Paris prepared to leave the city for their long sojourn in the country. Lecourt closed his house and took a house on the Dordogne. Mlle. Rochereau went down to stay.

She noticed that away from Paris, her fiancé seemed kinder, more thoughtful. They swam and boated on the river, walked in the parkland, lazed on the terrace.

There were three horses in the stables. Two they would ride, the other, old and docile, would be harnessed to a little trap they used for picnics. The countryside was drowsy and hot. In the fields the corn ripened in the sun. Birds sang lethargically. It was an incongruous setting for the terror which was to come.

One Thursday night about midnight, Lecourt was awakened by the sound of thundering hooves. He left his bed and went to the window.

Through the tree-dotted grassland beyond the house he saw a horse being galloped at speed. He recognized his own horse but not the dark, crouching figure on its back.

A dark figure

Quickly he dressed and ran round to the stable to wake the groom. In the stable yard they found the panting, sweating horse. It was saddled and bridled, but no one was there.

On the next night, Edith Rochereau was awakened by shouting. The moon was full and its light streamed into the room. She looked through the window and saw her fiancé, fully dressed, running across the terrace and into the parkland.

Following about a hundred yards behind was Favreau, the groom. Lecourt was shouting as he ran. Then among the shadows of a group of trees the girl saw a movement. There was a horse standing beneath the branches of an elm and on its back was a dark figure.

As Lecourt approached the horse began to move. It wheeled away and cantered in a wide arc through the trees. Then at full gallop it swung towards the running man.

As though watching some dreadful drama on a floodlit stage, Edith Rochereau stood transfixed at her window.

A scream

The white moonlight brought the figures into razor-sharp focus. She could see that the horse was being ridden by an old woman.

Arms outstretched, Favreau rushed to protect his master, but he was too late. With a scream, the man fell under the deadly hooves as the horse galloped back towards the trees.

Even as the groom bent over, the moonlit grass was being stained a dark red.

They carried Paul Lecourt back into the house and called a doctor but there was nothing he could do. The horse was found wandering riderless in a field of corn.

On August 8, 1912, one day before the anniversary of the death of his aunt, Lecourt was buried in the churchyard at the village of Clere.

Marie Giscard had kept her promise.

WARNING OF DISASTER—FROM AN INVISIBLE HAND!

Mystery force told of a pilot's death . . .

Dishes shattered . . . a breadknife exploded into five pieces . . . a table-top split in half—all the work of an invisible force. And it happened at the precise moment a man died, his plane shot down in flames hundreds of miles away.

UNDER THE moon-scudding clouds, a lone Hurricane fighter

droned over the French coast after a sortie on German munitions convoys.

There had been five in the flight, but the gunfire had been unexpectedly savage and Sergeant-Pilot Frank Williams had seen three of his colleagues swing towards earth on their parachutes, and the other burst in a cascade of fire in the midst of a green field.

The shore batteries of Dieppe opened up as the fighter flew over. Flak sprayed round the wings and a shell plunged deep into the fuselage, spinning the Hurricane over and sending it down to explode amid the shingle and barbed wire of the beach.

The date was July 5, 1943, and the time 11:30 P.M. when Frank Williams died. It was three days before Fighter Command released news of his death.

Yet, independently, inexplicably, six families living around his home in Cardiff had been warned that disaster had struck.

No surprise

At the instant his aircraft hit the beach, things began to happen in the homes of those who knew and loved Frank Williams. News of his death was received with grief and tears, but it was not received with surprise.

Researchers have, over the years, built up a complete dossier of the events of that night. They have co-ordinated fact with surmise, collected detailed statements. The more they know of the death of Sergeant-Pilot Williams, the less they understand.

The night of July 5 was warm and sultry. People walked the streets of Cardiff for a last breath of air before black-out was clamped over the windows.

At a house in Oakfield Street there was a farewell party: Sergeant Walter Owen was going back to the war. His sister was at the party. Her husband should have been there, too, but he had been recalled unexpectedly three days earlier. He was a Hurricane pilot.

The party decided to toast Walter Owen. His wife produced a bottle of champagne—one of three they had kept to celebrate the end of the war.

"Let's give him a good send-off," she said. She produced her best wine glasses and handed them round.

"I'd like to give a toast too," Sergeant Owen said. "I give you a toast to Frank Williams, who should have been here tonight."

Violent crash

They stood with glasses raised. There was a sharp report, a tinkling of glass—and champagne showered over Owen's right arm.

He stared unbelievingly at the stem of the glass he still held in his fingers. It had been neatly sliced off an inch above his hand.

There was silence. The party spirit had disappeared like smoke up a chimney. Seconds later, there was another violent crash. A mirror plunged to the floor, shattering across the room.

The sturdy hook which had held the mirror to the wall was bent down as if by some invisible hand. As they stood, frozen with shock, the mantlepiece clock struck half past eleven.

Invisible force

In Penarth Road, the other side of the town, Mrs. Gwen Watkins was asleep and dreaming. In her dream she saw the face of her nephew Frank Williams. In one sequence he was smiling. In the next, subdued and sad, he told her he was going away. Then he vanished.

Next door to the Williams' house in Richmond Street, a middle-aged couple, John and Louise Hall, were preparing to go upstairs to bed. It had been a quiet night with no air raids. The clock on the sideboard struck eleven thirty. The next moment it had slipped forward and crashed at John's feet. Instantaneously, his wife, who was in the kitchen, saw a pile of dishes swept out of a cupboard by some powerful and invisible force.

In a house further up the street, another relation of Frank Williams was sitting at the kitchen table writing a letter to his own son serving in the Far East.

Widow unaware

He, too, heard a clock strike 11:30 P.M. Then the silent calm was brutally smashed. He cowered away as a steel bread-knife, lying on the top of a cupboard, viciously exploded into five pieces. Then, with a nerve-grating wrench, the tabletop on which he was leaning split noisily across the middle.

But it was left to Sergeant Williams' young widow, Jessie, to provide the most baffling evidence in the case. The next morning still unaware that her husband was dead, she busied herself in the tiny garden behind the house.

One rose grew

The ground was poor. The previous year, Frank had planted three rose trees but they had quickly died and now stood like dry sticks in a border alongside the lawn.

Suddenly a brush-stroke of vivid color caught her eye. She stared unbelievingly at one of the withered bushes.

Growing firmly from a twig was one magnificent red rose. . . .

FACE TO FACE WITH A CREATURE FROM SPACE!

Were these visitors mapping the earth?

Out of the night sky loomed a yellow-reddish light. And then, incredibly, the four teenagers saw a creature the size of a human, but with bat-like wings. Experts are convinced that it came from space . . . and is only one of many to have visited the earth recently.

"THERE'S NO DOUBT—it was a light. A reddish-yellow light coming out of the sky at an angle of about 60 degrees. As it came towards the ground it seemed to hover more slowly. It disappeared behind the trees. Then, after a few seconds, this creature shambled out. We all saw it . . ."

The policeman on night duty in the country station took the facts down carefully and dutifully. It was difficult—the boy who had beaten on the station door at 1 A.M., poured out his story in a fearful, semi-coherent rush. As he spoke, he glanced nervously at the windows.

It was a fantastic story. Many policeman would have sent the boy packing, but this one didn't. Instead he took down the facts. His report read more like the synopsis of a science-fiction thriller than the nightly log of a country police station. For the 17-year-old John Flaxton and his three friends had, if their story was true, come face to face with a creature from another world.

Dark with shadow

The story has been analyzed by space scientists and researchers. John Flaxton and his friends have been cross-examined. They stick to their tale; and certainly the white-faced terror in which they arrived at the local police station could hardly have been faked.

From them, researchers have got the most complete, detailed and inexplicable report yet about the things which come out of the night sky.

The evening of November 10, 1962, was sharp and ice-clear. The moon shed an encouraging sliver of light across a lonely stretch of England's Kent countryside. And the three youths and a girl who walked along the country road were glad of the extra brightness.

Rigid with fright

They had been to a dance in a nearby town and had missed the last bus home to the village of Saltwood. Their footsteps rattled in the frosty air. The trees and hedges were dark with shadow. They were all young and a little nervous. They would be glad when the next rise was breasted and their village came in sight.

John Flaxton had his arm linked with the girl's, helping her up the slope which led to the clump of trees which concealed Slaybrook Corner.

They were talking about the dance. The girl looking nervously at the approaching trees, turned to the sky for reassurance and stopped, rigid with fright. Out of the sky loomed a reddish-yellow light.

It swung lower. The four scurried under the shelter of a tall hedge. As the light came towards the ground it hovered, about ten feet up. Then it moved again, and vanished behind a clump of trees.

Nowhere to hide

But the terror was only just beginning. Suddenly a bright golden light appeared in the field alongside the road. The girl began to run; the others followed, shouting in panic. But there was nowhere to hide.

John Flaxton remembers every second of the next ten minutes. "It was about eight yards away, floating about ten feet from the ground. It seemed to move along with us. It stopped when we stopped, as if it was observing us.

"The light was oval, about 15 to 20 feet across, with a bright solid core. Then it vanished behind some more trees. We heard a soft bump."

There was a metallic scraping sound, as if a hatch were opening. There was a rasping rattle. Then silence. The four teenagers stood by the roadside. They could not imagine what might happen next.

Then with a rustle of undergrowth, a creature appeared out of the wood and moved into the moonlit field towards the road.

"A dreadful thing"

"It was black, about the size of a human, but it had no head. It appeared to have bat wings on either side," said John Flaxton. "It came stumbling towards us. It was the most dreadful thing I have ever seen."

Understandably, they did not stay to see any more. John's last backward glance, as they rounded Slaybrook Corner, was of the creature standing motionless by the hedge which bounded the road.

As the story spread through the neighborhood, hundreds

of sightseers descended on Saltwood Village. Hysterical tales of shadowy shapes and winking lights flooded the area.

But amid the welter of scare stories and reports of strange lights in the sky, a definite pattern began to emerge. The description of the creature tallied with that of nearly half the total of 153 "flying saucer pilots" seen in Europe and America in the past 30 years.

The only route

The Unidentified Object Research Organization are convinced the lights and the creature came from a flying saucer. The descriptions from the teenagers tally with a spate of sightings over the past three years.

But why should flying saucers single out this remote village? This is where we get the most hair-raising fact of all.

Recently, Aime Michel, a French acoustics expert, put forward the theory that men from space were mapping the earth, traveling along fixed orbital lines. From hundreds of "sightings" a complex map of "saucer routes" has been compiled.

Yet there is only one route which crossed the British Isles. It comes over the Channel and across to the North Atlantic. And Saltwood Village is exactly on this route. . . .

BATTLE IN THE NIGHT—BETWEEN GHOST ARMIES!

Sounds of war returned . . . nine years after . . .

Two women peered frightened from the balcony of a small French hotel while the noise of battle rolled and

*reverberated round them. The countryside was still—
yet they were hearing sounds which, minute-for-minute,
matched those of an invasion battle fought nine years
earlier.*

THROUGH THE haze of a summer night came the heavy crackle
of gunfire, the moan of aircraft and the shouts of wounded
men.

Ten thousand Allied troops tumbled from landing-craft on
to the beaches of Dieppe.

About a mile east of Dieppe, two women stood together
on the balcony of a small hotel, peering through the darkness
towards the sea. They were tense and frightened. The noise
of battle rolled and reverberated around them.

The date was August 1951, but minute-for-minute, the
sounds they heard matched the bitter battle fought nine
years ago to the day, when the Allies made their daring raid
to probe the strength of German troops.

Can the human mind break through the time barrier and
visit the past?

Uncanny sound

Occasionally people claim to have seen and heard the re-
enactment of past events, but never has such an experience
been so well-documented and investigated as the night history gave a second showing to one of its classic moments.

It was witnessed by two Englishwomen on holiday in
Dieppe with their children. One was the wife of a British
Member of Parliament, the other her sister-in-law. For 13
years they have shunned publicity. Only if their real names
were kept secret would they agree to tell their incredible
story.

It had been a hot day and they had spent it on the beach.
At 11 P.M. feeling healthily tired, the women, who we can

call Ann and Mary, went up to the second floor sea-facing room that they shared.

At 4 A.M. Mary awoke, aware of an uncanny sound. First she thought it was far-off thunder heralding a storm. Then it grew louder, more insistent, and seemed to be coming from the beach.

Sound of battle

There was shouting and distant rumbling. Then Ann woke, too. "What is that noise?" she asked. For a while they lay in the dark listening, as the noise grew louder still.

Mary later told researchers: "It sounded like a roar which ebbed and flowed. We could distinctly hear the sounds of cries, shouts and gunfire."

Ann had served in the W.R.N.S. There was no doubt in her mind what the noise was: it was the sound of battle.

They got out of bed and went cautiously out on to the balcony outside their window. Nothing moved; there was not even a car on the road leading to the beach. There were no troops; they could hear the crackle of exploding star-shells but could not see their dazzling light.

Pitch of violence

Yet the noise was real enough: the crescendo of cries and shouts, the screech of shells passing overhead.

At 4:50 A.M. the noise stopped abruptly and started again 15 minutes later. This time it reached a new pitch of violence. Aerial bombardment was intensified, dive-bombers droned and whined over the dunes. Tanks rattled and rumbled past the hotel—but there were no score marks on the road.

But why, wondered the women, had nobody else in the hotel not heard the infernal din?

Until 7 A.M. the noise of battle continued in varying degrees of intensity. Then the last shot was fired, the sound of tanks and aircraft receded into the distance. The birds began to sing.

Trick of time

Later they asked other guests if they had been disturbed by tumult in the night, but no one had. Reluctantly, the women reached the conclusion that in some inexplicable way, some weird trick of time, they had tuned in to a battle fought nine years earlier.

They each wrote a separate account of what they had heard—and sent it to the Society for Psychical Research.

Intrigued investigators followed up their accounts and were able to work out a time-table of events which could be compared with the time schedule of the actual invasion.

Incredibly, it was found that the lulls, attacks, and aircraft and transport movements corresponded precisely. And another thing: no detailed history of the Dieppe raid was published until some years after the women's experience.

Was there any logical explanation? At first, researchers considered the possibility of the sounds coming from a nearby cinema in the area.

What purpose?

Could it have been army maneuvers, artillery practice—or even defective waterpipes? But these solutions were ruled out—for no one else in the area had heard the commotion.

The women were interviewed by several researchers. One reported: "They struck me as sane, well-balanced women with no tendency to add color to their accounts. I think the experience must be rated as genuine psychic phenomenon. After all, what other explanation is there?"

There are, of course, other theories: Did some strange

"time machine" click into reverse? Did the women somehow break into a "fourth dimension" where long-dead sounds are preserved?

But investigators are agreed on one thing. The women are of undoubted integrity; they have shunned publicity rather than sought it.

What purpose could they have had in inventing the eerie, unaccountable events of that strange August night?

SHE SAW A MURDER IN HER MIND'S EYE

And told police where to find the body . . .

Madame Edith Morel did not know old Andre Girard and had never been near his farm. Yet she knew he had ben murdered and by whom. Following her instructions, police found the body—and the man responsible for the crime.

IT WAS just after midday when old Andre Girard went through his farmyard and out into the sloping meadows to select half a dozen sheep for market. When he hadn't returned by mid-afternoon, his wife and son went out to look for him.

When he was still missing at nightfall, they called the police.

The next day, three detectives from Limoges arrived in the tiny farming village of Osty, in mid-western France, to help the local gendarmes with the search.

No one expected anything very drastic. Old Andre, who farmed with his sons, the biggest holding in the village, was over 70. Perhaps the strenuous life of full-time farming had at last proved too much.

Not even the detectives seriously considered murder. It took a complete stranger sitting 200 miles away in a Paris apartment to tell them that.

Found nothing

She had never heard of Andre Girard, never knew of his existence. Yet she knew exactly where his body was lying and who was responsible for his death.

The strange events surrounding the death of Andre Girard began on October 4, 1938. Detective Paul Marchal and two colleagues had arrived in Osty from Limoges expecting at the most a morning's work. With the two local gendarmes and half a dozen villagers, they walked Girard's land, searched woodland and prodded poles into nearby ponds. They found nothing.

In the afternoon, Marchal went round the village trying to build up a picture of Girard's last movements. The wife of a laborer who worked for the old man said she had seen Girard setting off up the fields when she took her husband his midday meal. There had been no one with him.

Police baffled

Further searches and investigations continued for three days, but with no result. What was first thought to be a country mishap began to assume the proportions of a mystery. News of Andre Girard's death got into the provincial papers.

That was how the case came to the notice of Dr. Eugene Favreau, director of Paris' *Institut Metapsychique.*

He telephoned the police bureau in Limoges and asked if he could help: the case seemed tailor-made for an experiment he had long wanted to try.

The police admitted they were baffled by the disappear-ance. They would welcome Dr. Favreau's cooperation, so long as he was reasonably unobtrusive.

"When can we expect you?" asked the Prefect.

"I will not be coming," answered Dr. Favreau. "I can op-erate quite well from here. All I ask is that you send me some small possession belonging to the missing man."

Mystified, the Prefect agreed. He passed on the request to Marchal, who obtained a small green scarf from Girard's wife. This was mailed to Paris.

Against his will

Next day, Dr. Favreau took the scarf to the apartment of Madame Edith Morel, a clairvoyant who had showed as-tonishing evidence of possessing a sixth sense—an extra-sensory perception.

Taking the scarf from its box, Dr. Favreau asked: "Can you tell me anything about this, and about its owner?" He gave no other clue; said nothing about the disappearance.

Madame Morel put the scarf on a table and looked at it for perhaps half a minute. "It belongs to an old man," she said. "He wears rough clothes—a tweed coat and cord trousers.

"He has been taken away against his will. I see him walk-ing up steep fields and into a forest. He is being taken along narrow paths. There is a man with him—a man in a black coat and hat."

"And the old man?" asked Dr. Favreau. "Is he alive or dead?"

"He's dead," said Madame Morel.

"Where is he?"

Body found

"Near Limoges," said Madame Morel. She had never been within 100 miles of the place, yet she gave the precise spot where the man's body was lying. She described a complex route of paths which would lead to the body, huddled in a tiny clearing.

"What about the man who took him into the woods?" asked Dr. Favreau, but Madame Morel could tell little about him, except, he had a white face, and one finger was missing on his hand.

The amazing interview ended. Dr. Favreau drew up a detailed report and sent it to the police.

On October 10, Detective Marchal led a search party into the dense woods skirting Girard's land. He had a map drawn by Dr. Favreau from Madame Morel's instructions. They followed the paths and finally came to a small clearing. There, huddled in the way exactly described by Madame Morel, was the body of Andre Girard. He had been shot in the back, obviously from close range.

Never told him

On the morning of October 15, an unemployed car mechanic named Marc Barbier was arrested in the nearby town of St. Sulpice on robbery charges.

He was middle-aged, pale, and was lacking the little finger of his left hand. In a battered brief case, police found a gun.

Barbier made a full confession: he had been sleeping in the meadow when Girard surprised him. He had taken the old man into a wood to rob him, and fired when Girard tried to get away.

In a statement Barbier said: "I could not see how anyone

could have laid the blame on me. At least tell me, how you found out."

Marc Barbier was executed in January 1939. The police never told him the strange tale of how he had been caught. They could hardly believe it themselves.

VOICE FROM THE GRAVE TOLD WHY AIRSHIP CRASHED

Only dead pilot could give these vital clues...

An incredible and uncannily accurate dossier came before the committee investigating the R. 101 disaster. It told in tragic detail how the R. 101 died—as only the man at the controls could have seen it. Yet that man had been killed in the crash. Had he returned from the grave to give the vital clues to the cause of the disaster?

ON THE NIGHT of October 5, 1930, Britain's largest and most dangerous airship lay in a French cornfield burning in the rain.

Earlier in the day, the R.101, the huge and lethal flying sausage of steel and hydrogen had begun a trip to India which it was hoped would clear the airship of charges of being a dangerous and impractical method of transport.

Instead it crashed. Its puny engines were powerless against the buffeting of the wind, the lashing of the rain. Air Marshals and statesmen died at their white-clothed table in the ornate dining saloon.

Of the 56 passengers 48, including the crew, perished in the flames. The remaining eight, critically burned, were hurried to hospitals.

Yet within a few days, there was a complete dossier of the

last hours of the R.101 locked in a desk at the Air Ministry in London. It contained information which only an experienced airship technician could give. It told down to the last tragic detail, why and how the R.101 died.

And it came from Flight-Lieutenant H. Carmichael Irwin, captain of the R.101 . . . and who was killed instantly in the crash.

Listened to the dead

There is seeming insurmountable evidence that he returned, two days after his death, to give an uncanny account of the tragedy.

For on October 7, three people came out of a house in London's South Kensington, with a book of shorthand notes and an unshakable conviction that for the past half hour they had been listening to a voice from the dead.

They had attended a seance given by the internationally famous medium Mrs. Eileen Garrett. Sitting at a table in the darkened room were Mr. Harry Price, Director of the National Laboratory for Psychical Research, his secretary, Miss Ethel Beenham, and journalist Mr. Ian Coster.

Soon after the session began, Mrs. Garrett slumped in a chair and appeared to be unconscious. Then in a strangely masculine voice she began to speak:

The last hours

"I am Flight-Lieutenant H. Carmichael Irwin, Captain of the R.101."

Then, with an extraordinary wealth of technical detail, the voice began to describe the airship's last hours.

"For heaven's sake, give this to them," it said. "The whole bulk of the dirigible was entirely too much for her engine capacity . . ." The voice spoke rapidly, disjointedly, and Miss Beenham's pencil raced to take down the words.

"Explosion caused by friction in an electric storm. Flying at too low an altitude and could never rise. Load too great for so long a flight. Same with S.L.8. Tell Eckener."

This last sentence was particularly puzzling. But later a search of German airship records revealed that S.L.8 was a German airship which had been built by a man named Eckener.

Moment of disaster

The voice continued: "Cruising speed was poor and the ship was swinging badly. Severe tension of the fabric caused chafing, particularly on the starboard strakes."

Mrs. Garrett had absolutely no technical knowledge of airships. How could she have known that "strakes"—normally a nautical term—was used by airship pilots to describe the side framework of their craft?

As the voice continued, more and more technical details were revealed—showing that whoever was talking had an intimate knowledge of airships and their construction.

Slowly, the narration reached the moment of disaster: "Weather bad for long flight. Fabric waterlogged and ship's nose is down. Impossible to rise. Cannot trim. For two hours, tried to rise, but elevator is jammed. Almost scraped the roofs at Achy. Kept to the railway line.

Hadn't a chance

"At inquiry they will find that the superstructure of the envelope contained no resilience and there was far too much weight in the envelope.

"From the beginning of the trouble, I knew we hadn't a chance."

Mrs. Garrett moved in her chair. The amazing seance was over. Afterwards she could remember nothing of what happened in her trance.

When the notes were transcribed an uncanny picture of what must have happened aboard the doomed airship began to emerge . . . if it was true. But was it?

Harry Price took a copy to an officer at the Royal Airship Works at Cardington, Bedford, where the R.101 was built. He was astounded.

Equally impressed

"This is an amazing document," he told Price. "It contains more than 40 references to highly technical and confidential details. The idea that anyone at the seance could have obtained this information beforehand is absurd."

Flight-Lieutenant William Wood, an airship pilot and friend of Irwin was equally impressed by the report.

He said: "I was interested to hear that the voice spoke quickly and disjointedly—that's how Irwin spoke. It was often difficult to tell what he said."

So it was that the most unorthodox report ever compiled on a disaster found its way on to the table of the official committee of inquiry set up to probe the disaster.

"I'll never know"

The committee heard from eye-witnesses and from experts who had tried to reconstruct the last moments of the airship. Then the chairman rose hesitantly, Irwin's testimony in his hand.

He began to read; and the members of the tribunal could hardly believe their ears. The report tied in perfectly with the evidence they had heard—and filled in a wealth of detail.

Reluctantly the report was disregarded, although the official findings were exactly what Irwin had predicted: there was too much weight aboard which had affected buoyancy.

Years later, Eileen Garrett was still perplexed by her experience. "Was it really Irwin?" she was asked recently. "I don't know," she answered. "And I never will."

ONLY ANIMALS KNEW A CITY WAS DOOMED

In fear they waited for death at dawn . . .

While the Yugoslav city of Skoplje was sleeping under the pale dawn sky, the animals of the area were going berserk with inexplicable fear. Nothing appeared to be wrong, yet all living things, except the human population, seemed to know that the earth was about to open.

NIKOLA MARINKO and his wife Valentina, were awakened at 5 A.M. on July 26 to hear a scuffling and fluttering in the living room below.

On his way downstairs, Marinko glanced out of the landing window: the provincial Yugoslav city of Skoplje was sleeping under the pale dawn sky.

As he entered the living room, the noise stopped. Feathers fluttered around the room. In a cage swinging near the window, the family's canary lay dead. It had obviously beaten itself to death in a frenzied struggle to get out of the cage.

Nikola Marinko was not a particularly imaginative man, but he felt instinctively that something was about to happen. He woke his two children and told them to get dressed. Then the family left the house and climbed the sloping plain away from the city.

Throughout Skoplje birds and animals were panicking. Inexplicably, they knew that disaster was near. Only the Marinko family heeded the warning.

Day of horror

Then at 5:17 A.M. the solid buildings of Skoplje were rattled like dice in a box. With a sound of thunder the city collapsed as one of the most terrible earthquakes of the century hit the area.

More than 1,000 Yugoslavs died in that day of horror last July. Yet many might have lived if only they had taken note of the animals' behavior.

For half an hour before the earthquake reduced Skoplje to rubble, patrolling policemen had noticed that there was not a bird or a pigeon to be seen in the streets.

In the central police headquarters, night staff were disturbed by the inconsolable howling of two tracker dogs kept in the station. Frantically the animals leaped at windows seeking a means of escape.

Nothing seemed wrong, yet every living thing in Skoplje—except the 120,000 people who were soon to find themselves homeless—seemed to know that the earth was about to open.

Roared and bellowed

In the city zoo, keepers and officials were awakened at 4:30 A.M. by what was later described as a "concert of terror." Animals were going berserk. Lions and tigers paced their cages roaring and bellowing.

Elephants, trumpeting wildly, rushed at the fence of their enclosures seeking to escape. Officials, first thinking that someone must have broken in and scared the animals, could find nothing wrong.

Then with a desperate rush, a female elephant tore down

73

a line of steel railings and galloped away across a lawn strewing bushes and ornamental shrubs in her wake. A keeper who tried to calm her was injured.

Endless seconds

The superintendent ran back to his house for a gun. Then an uncanny thing happened: as if by a signal the animals became strangely quiet. The stampeding elephant stopped in its tracks and allowed itself to be led back to the cages. It was as though the animals had resigned themselves to their fate. Then, a minute later, devastation came to Skoplje.

For endless seconds nothing could be heard but the crash of collapsing buildings. The five-story Hotel Macedonia swayed from side to side, before tumbling its 180 bedrooms and their occupants into the street.

Bricks shot through the air as if fired by cannon. Dazed survivors wandered through the streets. A man babbled: "I thought it was the hydrogen bomb." A six-story building shrank in size as the earth swallowed up the two lower floors.

Birds returned

One of the most crippling disasters was the total collapse of three apartment buildings housing the town's doctors and their families.

Rescue planes circling the city could see the red eyes of kindling fires shining through the dust cloud hanging over Skoplje.

Soon medical teams began to pour into the stricken city, trucks brought in desperately needed water.

At least 80 per cent of buildings were destroyed or badly damaged and all services disrupted; over 100,000 people were made homeless and 2,000 injured—all in a few seconds.

The next day, the first few birds returned to the stricken

city. How did they know that trouble was in the air? Was it some mysterious sixth sense?

Uncanny sense

Some experts believe that centuries of experience have left animals with a memory imprint of danger at hand.

If humans ever had this sense they now seem to have lost it—cushioned against adversity by policemen, doctors and insurance companies.

Another theory is that animals are warned by a build-up in electrical pressure, or have a built-in "early warning system."

This uncanny sense animals have is hard to believe. But it is harder to discredit. Whatever the reason, animals *can* tell when we humans are in danger.

We can ignore their warning, but—as at Skoplje—at our peril.

PANIC AT SEA—AS A GHOST WALKED THE DECK

Did it hound this crack German sub to its doom?

Throughout its life, the German submarine UB-65 was under the curse of a ghost. Its victims committed suicide or died in inexplicable ways. And at the final reckoning when the sub was torn apart by a mystery explosion, it was standing on the deck—and smiling.

WHITE FEATHERS of foam flicked from the oily steel plates

as the shark-like hull of the German submarine UB-65 emerged from the North Sea.

She was sleek, deadly, and for a boat built in 1915, modern. But her crew hated her.

Shaken and demoralized, they had petitioned the German High Command for a transfer to another ship. Several men were in naval prisons for refusing to return after leave.

For she was jinxed. Five men had died making her, and half a dozen others had perished in inexplicable ways.

And now, on this September morning in 1916, as she rose to recharge batteries after a night of hounding Allied shipping in the Dover Straits, came the incident that established the UB-65 saga as a disturbing and macabre classic of the sea.

Chilling silence

For as the U-boat came surging and dripping out of the gray water, the captain at his periscope and two look-outs at observation hatches saw it quite clearly: a man was standing motionless, arms folded, on the submarine's bows.

There was a jolt of chilled silence, broken as a lookout shrieked: "It's come back! It's standing there."

The ghost of the UB-65 was to withstand scepticism, official High Command denial, even exorcism. It was to stay with the ship throughout its ill-starred career. And eventually it was to destroy her.

There is no logical explanation for the events which sent morale in the German Number Two Submarine Flotilla to rock-bottom during the last years of the First World War.

Face to face

The ghost, seen by dozens, both officers and men, was said to be that of her First Lieutenant, killed with five ratings when a torpedo blew up as UB-65 was taking on war supplies. But it was not until September 1916 that it came face to face with its victims.

Right from the beginning, the UB-65 was the odd ship out. While she was being built, two men were crushed by a girder slipping from its slings, and three others died from engine-room fumes.

On the first day of the sub's test cruise, an officer making a routine inspection of the hull deliberately walked overboard and was never seen again. On the first dive, the boat refused to surface, and lay on the sea bed for 15 hours as men struggled to repair her waterlogged batteries.

Hushed up

From then on, it was a roll-call of disaster. At Bruges, in Belgium, the torpedo blew up while being maneuvered into a firing tube, and Admiral Ludwig von Schroder of the German High Command, sent the U-boat into dry dock for examination.

The crew was given leave and a watch remained on board. The same night, the petty officer of the watch dashed into the captain's cabin and shouted: "I saw it. It's come on board—the ghost of the first officer. Pederson saw it too . . . standing in the bows with its arms folded."

But the incident was hushed up, and dismissed by the High Command as the effect of battle fatigue on a raw, frightened crew.

The submarine was sent out again. Everything went well and it began to look as though the jinx had been shaken off. She torpedoed and sank an Allied ship.

But it was on the following morning, as she surfaced for battery recharging, that the horrified lookouts saw the apparition in the bows.

"It's come back," echoed through the ship. "It's standing there, arms folded just like Pederson saw it."

Shocked and frightened

Knowing that he must break the spell, the commander opened the conning tower, cupped his hands, and called: "You there!"

Slowly, claimed witnesses, the figure in the bows turned towards the watchers. It had the face of the dead lieutenant. Quickly the captain slammed the tower lid and put the ship into a dive. But they couldn't get away: the ghost was riding with them.

Spines tingled, as soft laughter was heard throughout the submarine.

Shocked and frightened the crew turned the craft for home. An Allied bombing raid was in progress as they docked in Bruges. A shell splinter pierced the conning tower and killed the commander.

This time the High Command had little alternative but to take some action. Admiral Schroder had the vessel docked, the crew given compassionate leave. Then a chaplain conducted a service of exorcism.

But the ghost of the UB-65 had further work to do. In May 1918, off Cape Finisterre, a leading gunner went mad and killed himself; an engineer developed a high fever and died during the night; the next morning, a petty officer jumped overboard to his death.

No sign of life

All three men claimed to have seen the ghost.

Back in Bruges, the whole crew was replaced while the ship was refitted. In July, under a new command, UB-65 moved out into the Atlantic seeking convoys near the Irish coast. The ghost, it seems, went too.

What panic it caused, what disaster it wrought, will never

be known. But on the morning of July 10, the American submarine L-2 spotted a craft on the horizon; it was UB-65, drifting and apparently derelict. There was no sign of life.

The U.S. boat closed in, but before she could even fire a warning salvo, a violent explosion blotted out the target. The German submarine reared bow-first into the air and slid under the surface.

Just before she sank, the American commander and two of his officers saw through binoculars the figure of a man standing motionless in the bows.

His arms were folded across his chest. And he was smiling.

THE UNSEEN HAND THAT TERRORISED A FAMILY

Furniture flew, books fell—yet no one was there!

While observers watched, the furniture in the tiny bedroom performed a macabre dance. A dresser rocked; drawers were thrown about. Never before had such phenomena been seen by so many independent witnesses. For three months they continued—and then ended as mysteriously as they had begun.

ON A WARM September evening in 1952, several hundred people crammed the narrow pavements of Byron Street, a narrow, normally quiet thoroughfare in the north of England town of Runcorn.

As midnight approached, the knots of people grew. They spilled through the open front door of Number One, and up the stairs. Behind the closed door of the front bedroom, two shivering boys lay in bed and waited. The crowd fell silent. They were awaiting the arrival of the Runcorn poltergeist.

On the landing outside the room was a strange assortment of people: church ministers, a radio recording team, a group of scientists with infra-red cameras. They, too, were waiting.

As midnight struck, the atmosphere perceptibly chilled, and the sound of violence rent the air.

The door was opened. Powerful torch beams illuminated a scene which had become a spine-chilling classic of inexplicable phenomena.

Police were told

Before the terrified gaze of the boys, the furniture was doing a macabre dance. A dresser beat itself against a wall, rocking violently; a cardboard box was rising vertically in the air; drawers were being flung across the room.

Never before or since have such happenings been seen by so many independent witnesses and chronicled with such scientific impartiality.

A Methodist minister, the Rev. W. H. Stevens, who witnessed the majority of the Byron Street phenomena, spoke for his colleagues when he said: "One doubts the evidence of one's senses in these matters."

Mr. Sam Jones, a widower, lived in the little terraced house with his daughter-in-law and his grandson John Glynn, aged sixteen.

The strange occurrences began in August 1952, and Mr. Jones thinking he was the victim of a practical joke, reported the matter to the police.

Shook and rocked

But it was not a joke. A local spiritualist medium claimed to have made contact with an "entity." Psychic researchers decided this was a case for thorough investigation.

And so on the evening of September 22 they moved in.

By now, John Glynn was so alarmed by the nightly occurrences that he had persuaded a friend, 18-year-old John Berry, to share the room with him. At 11:30 P.M. they retired to bed and the watchers began their vigil.

Soon after the light had been switched off and all was quiet, the dressing table creaked and then moved. It began to shake and rock. By this time several people had entered the room and others crowded the doorway and stairs.

The Rev. Stevens recalls what happened next: "I found a table had moved into the middle of the room. It was pushed back, and promptly moved out again about six feet.

Eerie climax

"Addressing the table, I said: 'If you can hear my voice, knock three times.' Immediately it began to shake vigorously three times. All in the room saw the rocking table with no one near it.

"The two boys were lying in bed on the far side of the room. I went to see if the table would rock of its own accord but it was firm on the floor."

Soon afterwards, the activity began again. Small articles left the dressing table and were flung across the floor—books, ornaments, an alarm clock. A cloth on the table was ripped from top to bottom. A drawer was thrown out and its contents tipped on the bed.

The evening ended in eerie climax: John Glynn had his pillows snatched from under him, and then was thrown out of bed on to the floor. He declared he was pulled by force, and could not resist. And certainly he appeared terrified by the experience.

Indeed, a police sergeant, present during the incidents found John Glynn in a state of nervous collapse.

The policeman reported: "I have tried every method known to me, and believe me, those boys are not doing it. I am not strong enough to make that table dance about as it has done, and I am sure the boys could not do it."

Never caught

Night after night, the uncanny violence continued. Mr. Harold Crowther, a Runcorn farmer, and a staunch disbeliever in the supernatural, threw his overcoat on to the dressing table, remarking: "If you don't want it, give it back to me." Immediately, the coat was thrown back to him three times in succession.

The researchers naturally regarded the boys with suspicion. The room was searched every night and the boys were willing to submit to any test, even the tying of their hands and feet.

On one occasion, two scientists held John Glynn so that he could not touch anything. Under these circumstances, not only was the dressing table shaken violently, but on demand the shaking changed from the dressing table to a blanket chest.

Another time, while the lights were out, books and ornaments began to fly about causing deep scoring in the walls. When the lights were suddenly switched on, witnesses saw a box containing jigsaw puzzles rising upwards towards the ceiling.

The boys were lying in bed covered with blankets. After a few seconds, the box crashed to the ground—but not before photographs had been obtained.

The boys were never caught out in any trickery, although the lights were flashed constantly during the incidents, and the room was searched for mechanical devices.

Time will tell

Reluctantly, the researchers acknowledged that no human

activity appeared to be responsible for the uncanny activities in Byron Street. If it was fraud, then it was unbelievably skilled.

A report to the Society of Psychical Research reflected the bewilderment of the scientists over things they could not explain: "That these disturbances were not caused by human agency we are firmly convinced.

"During one particularly noisy period, we saw and obtained photographs of the dressing table several inches in the air.

"There is no logical explanation for such occurrences. For want of any better explanation we must attribute the disturbances to poltergeist phenomena."

By Christmas, 1952, the activities began to peter out. Eventually they stopped altogether. Crowds no longer gathered in the street, pressmen and scientists no longer kept vigil.

But whether the Runcorn poltergeist has really gone is a question only time can answer.

MYSTERY MESSAGES THAT BAFFLED TWO NATIONS

Did they really come from beyond the grave?

The experts were sure there was some trickery involved. For 20 years, they refused to believe that Leonora Piper could communicate with the dead. Yet they had to admit that her powers were uncanny. And, in the end, even the most confirmed sceptics came away convinced.

FOR TWENTY YEARS, they tried to trick Leonora Piper. They denounced her as a slick operator using some ingenious system, they spied on her, trailed her, and carried out a thousand tests.

And eventually, inevitably, they climbed down. They admitted, usually with the poorest grace, that for want of a better explanation, Leonora Piper could speak with the dead.

Until her death in 1954, Mrs. Piper provided the world with one of the most profound mysteries on psychical research.

Despite the most complex checks and precautions, experts found themselves unable to advance any theory about the uncanny way Mrs. Piper obtained information from the grave. Except, of course, the obvious one.

Professor William James, America's most celebrated psychologist, spent four years making a detailed study of Mrs. Piper's behavior. He went to her sittings and relentlessly questioned those who were there in his search for an accomplice.

No explanation

Eventually he admitted: "I now believe her to be in possession of a power as yet unexplained."

James first heard about Mrs. Piper from a relation who had attended a seance at her home in Boston, Massachusetts. He laughingly explained how unscrupulous mediums made a point of doing advance research on all their clients, how they employed agents to get information from tombstones, directories, and interviews with servants.

Eventually, intrigued by the extravagent claims made for Mrs. Piper, he went to a seance himself. He was surprised to find the medium was a tall pleasant-looking woman with little formal education, who could give no explanation for her powers.

Once in a trance, she was taken over by a "spirit control" who called himself "Dr. Phinuit," a dead French doctor who came from Metz. "Phinuit's" voice came through

Mrs. Piper as huskily masculine and tinged with a French accent.

After a few sessions, James was sure there was more than trickery involved. His mother, for example, had for some time been looking for a lost bank-book and he asked Mrs. Piper where it was.

A telegram

The medium described the place so exactly that the book was found instantly on the return home.

On another occasion, Mrs. Piper told James that his aunt, who was then living in New York, had died early that morning. "On reaching home," the professor noted, "I found a telegram saying: 'Aunt Kate passed away a few minutes after midnight.'"

Still, it was always possible that Mrs. Piper had in some way made a special investigation of the James family, so the professor brought a colleague to a sitting after Mrs. Piper was already in a trance.

She gave the correct names of the friend's parents, the illness from which his father died, and a whole array of other personal facts.

When the report reached the British Society for Psychical Research, there was cynical talk and comment about a man of James' intelligence being taken in so easily.

Detectives hired

An investigator was sent across the Atlantic to Boston to see Mrs. Piper at work. The man chosen was Dr. Richard Hodgson, a Cambridge don, who was making a life's work of exposing "psychic" wonders.

Soon after he landed in Boston, Hodgson had a sitting with Mrs. Piper. James introduced him as "Mr. Smith."

Mrs. Piper promptly told him his real name, the names of his brothers and sisters, that his father and youngest brother were dead and that as a child he enjoyed playing leapfrog with his cousin Fred.

That all this was true only served to convince Hodgson that Mrs. Piper was smarter than he had expected.

He hired detectives to trail her to see if she was doing surreptitious research; he deliberately sought out sitters who had no ties with Boston, or even New England. They were brought into the room only after she was in a trance and would leave before she came out of it.

Final test

After two years of constant search for fraud, Hodgson was nearly ready to admit Mrs. Piper's supernatural powers. But for a final test he planned to take her to a country where she had no friends, no family, no associates.

So in 1900, Mrs. Piper came to England. At the houses in which she stayed, entire new staffs of servants were engaged, her luggage was searched and she was watched constantly by members of the British Society for Psychical Research.

During her three months in Britain she gave 88 sittings and produced hundreds of detailed—and afterwards verified—facts about her sitters.

Many of them were incidents which were unknown to the sitters at the time of the seances.

By this time a new "control" had appeared on the scene. He was George Pellew, a young lawyer who had attended a Piper sitting and was killed soon afterwards.

Then one day "Phinuit" announced that George Pellew was present and wished to communicate.

Wore a mask

More than 30 of Pellew's friends and relations who came incognito to the sittings were recognized, and 100 others brought in deliberately to trip up the "spirit," were denounced.

Not only did "Pellew" remember friends, but also their opinions, occupations and habits. Once he translated a Greek phrase composed on the spot by a classical scholar—although Mrs. Piper knew no Greek.

He also reported accurately what his father, in another city was doing.

The Pellew sittings convinced many investigators that here at last was communication with the dead. Eventually, even the sternest critic was convinced.

He was Professor James H. Hyslop, of Columbia University, who, with the secret cooperation of Dr. Hodgson, attended 17 seances wearing a hood.

No theories

Without hesitation the medium told him his name, his father's name and gave him a wealth of detail about himself.

For the first time in his many years of unmasking frauds, Hyslop was bewildered. In the end, he said he believed he had actually spoken to the spirit of his dead father.

In 1910 Mrs. Piper discontinued the sittings on account of her health. She had survived the most prolonged investigation in the history of psychical research and yet she had no theories about her uncanny gifts. "I don't know what happens when I'm in a trance," she would say.

Leonora Piper died in a quiet Boston house, a bright-eyed old lady of 94. She took with her the secret which had convinced leading scientists of two nations that there is communication beyond the grave.

ORDEAL AT CHRISTMAS—AS A BOY VANISHED IN THE SKY!

How was he plucked from the face of the earth?

"Help, they've got me!" The screams of Oliver Thomas brought his family running out into the snow-flurried darkness. They stood powerless—for the cries came from above their heads. No one knows what took the boy away over the hills. But it never brought him back.

CHRISTMAS EVE, 1909, brought a fall of snow which drifted across the mountains of Wales and settled in their folds. In a farmhouse on a Brecon hillside, a dozen people sat round the kitchen range waiting to welcome in Christmas Day.

It was cold outside, and snowflakes flurried and beat against the window panes. Inside, the Thomas family and their friends poked chestnuts into the hot embers and sang the carols Grandfather Thomas thumped out lustily on the harmonium.

Sitting at the hearth-side, young Oliver Thomas, the 11-year-old son of hill farmer Owen Thomas, split open a brittle cooked nut with lazy satisfaction. Christmas was fun.

It was a comforting scene, a homely get-together which had become an annual event. How soon it was to change into a nightmare of raw terror, a mystery which has no parallel and certainly no solution.

It was the last Christmas Eve Oliver Thomas ever saw. For that night he was spirited away, silently, terrifyingly, over the hills, and never seen again.

Black and starless

There was no lack of witnesses to the disappearance of Oliver Thomas. A minister and his wife were there. So was the local veterinary surgeon, and an auctioneer from the nearby town.

All gave evidence at the inquest. None could advance any sensible theory. To this day the mystery remains as baffling as when Oliver Thomas vanished as literally and completely as if he had walked off the earth.

Everyone knew each other well round the Thomas fireside. They laughed, sang, and occasionally sat quietly in reminiscence.

Outside, the snow had stopped falling. It was about five inches deep, a soft fluffy blanket which lay as it fell. The wind had dropped and the night was black and starless.

A few minutes before 11 o'clock, Oliver's father noticed that the water bucket, standing near the sink, needed filling. He asked Oliver to run out to the well and bring in a bucket of fresh water.

He screamed

Oliver slipped on his boots and opened the back door and went out with the bucket into the yard. It was a duty he had done scores of times before—but he would never do it again.

About ten seconds after Oliver had closed the door behind him, the people in the kitchen heard him scream for help.

Chairs were overturned as the family and guests, headed by Owen Thomas, ran out of the back door.

The minister snatched up a paraffin lantern which sent its flickering rays out over the snowy yard. It was empty. But the air above was full of noise. Scream after scream chilled the little gathering.

They could hear Oliver shrieking: "They've got me! Help, help!"

Ended abruptly

Witnesses afterwards agreed that the cries came from overhead. Somewhere in the darkness Oliver Owen was in mortal fear. But of what?

The people below ran uncertainly and ineffectually to seek the answer. The screams grew fainter until they became inaudible. His family and friends stood in mute bewilderment; the wind sprang from the east and wailed among the mountains.

By the light of the lamp they found Oliver's footsteps in the snow. He had obviously gone about 75 feet across the yard towards the well, when his tracks ended abruptly.

The bucket lay on its side about fifteen feet away from the tracks. There were no other marks of any kind in the soft snow. Grief-stricken and frightened they returned to the house.

As bells in the valley chimed a Christmas welcome, the minister offered a brief prayer for the deliverance of Oliver Thomas, wherever he might be.

Gone for good

In the morning, police summoned from the nearby town of Rhayader, saw the footsteps and the bucket and were frankly skeptical.

They grappled the well with hooks, they searched the outbuildings and nearby slopes, they interrogated all present.

Reluctantly they were forced to the conclusion that Oliver Thomas had gone—upwards.

In the daylight it was seen clearly that the footprints had never reached the well and that the boy had not paused or turned aside. The only explanation was that he had been plucked bodily from the ground.

It was a tragic, lonely Christmas for those on the hillside farm. Hope tussled with grief and lost. By Boxing Day, it seemed pretty well certain that Oliver Thomas had gone for good.

But where, and how?

Just a memory

The cries fading away in the blackness overhead could not have been an illusion. They were the only clues to his sudden and dramatic disappearance.

Official records showed that no balloons were flying any-where in the country that winter night. Aeroplanes were still at the hedge-hopping stage and about as silent as a military band.

The boy weighed 75 pounds—far too much for any known bird to lift—and anyway he had screamed: "*They've got me.*" It was highly unlikely that a flock of birds would swoop down to carry him away.

Two days after Christmas, the snow fell again. It funneled down between the mountains and tossed a new white mantle over the Thomas farmyard.

It dissolved the last footsteps of Oliver Thomas, and filled in the dent where the bucket had lain.

There was nothing left. Nothing except the terrible memory of his screams fading and blending with the wind.

/

MIDNIGHT IN THE MUSEUM—THEN IN WALKED A GHOST

What was the secret of its mystery quest?

It was no ordinary caller who came to the museum late one Sunday night. When the caretaker stretched out his hand towards him, the man simply vanished. Then he returned later—and this time before the gaze of hardened cynics.

"EXCUSE ME, sir, do you want to see the curator?" The museum caretaker moved forward to peer at the strange old man rummaging busily through bookshelves.

It was approaching midnight one Sunday and no one had any right to be in the building. Instead of replying, the old man took down a heavy book and turned to look at his questioner.

He had an old face but curiously unlined. He had fluffy side-whiskers, and very little hair on top.

Not a very remarkable face, but the caretaker remembers every line of it from that day to this.

It was the face of a ghost.

In the autumn of 1953, the Yorkshire Museum in Museum Street, York, a little-known north of England institution, came into the world's headlines with a series of eerie and inexplicable happenings which rank as classics of their kind.

Heard footsteps

Of course, there have been ghost stories before, but rarely.

92

are they as well witnessed and documented as the events which occurred at the York Museum.

Less than half the dozen people who watched the apparition at work previously believed in the supernatural. A hardheaded doctor, known as a man who never believed anything he could not actually see, freely admitted the presence of something "not of this world."

The story began on Sunday, September 20, 1953, when a room in the museum was let for a religious meeting. After it was over, the caretaker, Mr. George Jonas, cleared away the chairs, locked the door and went down to the basement kitchen where his wife was waiting to go home.

At 11:40, they heard footsteps coming from the museum above. Thinking it was the curator going into his office, Mr. Jonas went upstairs to report that he was going off duty. But the man he saw crossing the landing outside the curator's office was someone he had never seen before.

Shuffled past

In a report for a scientific investigation, Mr. Jonas recalled his first thoughts. "I thought he was an odd-looking chap, because he was wearing drainpipe trousers, a frock coat and long side-whiskers. He walked with a stoop. I decided he must be an eccentric professor."

As Mr. Jonas approached, the man moved away. The caretaker asked if he could help, but the man did not answer, shuffled past and began to descend the stairs towards the library.

Now he was only a few feet away and Mr. Jonas saw the man's face clearly. He frowned, and muttered to himself: "I must find it, I must find it."

"It was queer," recalled Mr. Jonas later, "but of course I did not think about ghosts for one minute—he looked just as real as you and me. But I did not want him roaming around when the museum was shut, and anyway I wanted to lock up and catch my bus."

Touched his shoulder

By now they had reached the library. It was gloomy and Mr. Jonas switched on the lights. He noticed the man had on elastic-sided boots and a type of coat he had seen his grandfather wear.

Still muttering, the man went to the far end of the library, and, with the caretaker a few yards behind, stood between two tall book racks, lifting first one volume and then another from the shelves.

"I thought to myself that the game had gone on long enough," recalled Mr. Jonas. "I once again asked if he wanted the curator but got no reply. So, thinking he was deaf, I stretched out my right hand, to touch him on the shoulder.

"As my hand drew near, the man vanished and the book he was holding fell on to the floor."

The state of shock caused by his experience left his employers in little doubt that Mr. Jonas had seen *something*. He consulted his doctor, who was skeptical of the tale, but visited the library and witnessed some of the later events.

Experts moved in

Four weeks later, at exactly the same time, Mr. Jonas saw the apparition again. It walked across the landing, down the stairs, and through the closed doors of the library. This time the caretaker did not follow it.

What was the ghost looking for? By now the story of its activities had appeared in the world's papers. Reporters began to clamor round the museum gates every Sunday evening, seeking news of the latest incident.

By November, enough inexplicable events had occurred to

warrant a scientific investigation. A team equipped with cameras, tape recorders, and infra-red equipment moved into the library on the Sunday of November 15.

There, too, were Mr. Jonas, the doctor, and a local solicitor. As they entered the library all felt instinctively that someone was inside. Several men felt an icy rush of air.

Suddenly they heard the sound of pages being turned at the far end of the library. The men rushed across the room, only to hear a thud before they reached the vital shelf.

White hand

On the floor was a book, its pages still fluttering.

Three Sundays later, watchers saw the ghost at work again: as they stared, a shadow appeared to hover over a shelf. With a rasping sound, as though the books were tightly packed, a volume was drawn out, opened and dropped on the floor.

The whole shelf was immediately examined for thread, wires or any other devices which would indicate a hoax. But nothing was found.

The apparition only appeared once more. On the Sunday of February 7, 1954, a disembodied white hand was seen to pluck out a book and drop it on the floor.

Since then, the museum has returned to its placid backwater; no longer does its name mean anything to pressmen and news editors. But those who saw, and spoke to, the ghost, will never forget.

And one wonders, did it find what it sought, or will it one day return to the library to resume its macabre and mysterious quest?

DID A CURSE FROM THE GRAVE TAKE KITCHENER TO HIS DOOM?

Even the Queen sensed disaster was near . . .

A "double death" by fire and water . . . that was the curse directed against Kitchener. An Indian fakir made a similar prediction. Queen Alexandra, too, had a premonition of disaster—and even Kitchener himself seemed aware of the fate that awaited him.

ON AN EVENING in early summer a high black Rolls-Royce turned out of Clarence House, into London's stately Mall, and through the gates of Buckingham Palace.

There were few people about, but the handful of sightseers caught a glimpse of a tall stately figure in the back of the vehicle. Queen Alexandra, widow of King Edward VII, was making an urgent call on her son, King George V.

It was June 4, 1916. The next day Lord Kitchener, Britain's War Minister was leaving Scotland in the cruiser H.M.S. *Hampshire* for consultations in Russia.

And now, on his last evening in Britain, the Queen Mother came to her son with a startling request. "I have a sudden premonition that disaster awaits Lord Kitchener," she said. "I beg that his visit be postponed."

The King said he could not interfere. At 4 P.M. the next day in a rising gale Kitchener boarded the *Hampshire*—and was lost forever in the gray wastes of the North Sea.

"Double death"

The Queen was not the only one who knew he would die at sea. Kitchener himself knew it too. His many years in the East had given him a curious streak of mystic fatalism.

"I hate the sea," he once said, and often recalled a visit to an Indian fakir who had told him he would die while on the water.

And also in his mind was the Curse of the Mahdi, put on him years before in the Sudan when he sacked the white city of Omdurman, revenging the murder of General Charles Gordon.

Kitchener, the cold career soldier, said the Dervish prophets, would suffer a "double death" by fire and water. And so, nearly three decades later, it was to be.

During his last week-end alive, Kitchener had been thinking about this curse. He remarked to friends while strolling on the lawns of his house in Kent: "I am told I have *got* to be drowned."

Avenged in full

The battle of Omdurman was a battle of revenge. Thirteen years before, Mohammed ibn Abdella—"The Mahdi," self-appointed god of the Sudan Dervishes—had ordered the murder of General Gordon in the besieged town of Khartoum.

The Mahdi was dead and entombed in splendor in Omdurman, but the Dervish rebels fought on. Now they were to be smashed and Lord Kitchener had been chosen to do it.

Gordon had been Kitchener's hero and he was to avenge him in full. He razed the shrine of the Mahdi to the ground, burned the body, and had the bones thrown into the Nile.

He sent the skull to Cairo in a paraffin tin while he debated whether to have it converted into an ink-stand.

And he brought upon himself the curse—the inexplicable powers of evil, which even in death the Mahdi was said to wield.

To his doom

Outwardly it had little effect on him: he was made an earl, a freeman of the city of London and given a number of high commands.

When the First World War came, Kitchener became War Minister, his grim face glaring from recruitment posters.

Fate was closing in. Spectacular losses on the Russian front made liaison with the Czar imperative. German submarines lurked in the North Sea, but Kitchener had made up his mind: he would go to Russia.

When he reached Thurso on June 5, conditions were anything but summery. *Hampshire* rolled at her moorings, the wind was at storm force and a German submarine had been sighted some hours previously.

But Kitchener refused to allow the sailing to be postponed. He seemed anxious to hasten to his doom.

Glossed over

Hours later, the nation heard the stunning news: the cruiser had been torpedoed. Only a dozen sailors were saved. Kitchener was never seen again.

Unofficial versions of the disaster flooded the newspapers. One was that the body of Kitchener had been washed up on the coast of Norway and buried by fishermen.

Official statements derided this notion. An inquiry was held and the incident hurriedly glossed over.

And there the matter rested for ten years. Then excitement

reawakened: a journalist had arranged to have the Norwegian grave opened and the body brought to London for identification.

With high drama, the coffin entered England—where it was promptly seized by Scotland Yard and placed in a guarded mortuary until an inquest could be arranged.

Coffin opened

In the presence of a coroner, police, and noted pathologist Sir Bernard Spilsbury, the coffin was opened.

It was empty.

What had happened? No one officially knows, but the Home Office never denied a popular story that three top-ranking police officials had visited the mortuary the night before the inquest, abducted the body and had it cremated.

If this was so, Kitchener's body had indeed "died" twice —and the curse of the Mahdi had been completely and amazingly fulfilled.

HE HEARD THE HEART OF A GIRL FROM THE GRAVE

Dead 17 years, but she walked into mother's arms . . .

In a room locked and sealed, Harry Price met a girl called Rosalie. He held her hands, felt her pulse, asked her questions, watched her mother embrace her. Yet he knew that the child had been dead 17 years.

THE LARGE detached house in Wickham Road, Brockley, a smoky suburb in south London, was drab and needing a coat of paint. The garden was wild and untended.

As a nearby clock struck midnight, a man let himself out of the front door, walked hurriedly down the weedy path and hailed a passing cab.

As the taxi traveled along dim streets towards the West End, the man was writing rapid notes in a leather-bound folder. His hand shook as he wrote.

His name was Harry Price. He was the best known psychic investigator of his generation. But he was shaken and disturbed by what he had seen on that December night in 1937.

He had taken his usual painstaking precautions against the possibility of fraud. In a room, locked and sealed, he had met a child called Rosalie.

He had held her hands, listened to her heartbeat. Yet the child had died 17 years before.

Most baffling

It was Price's most amazing experience in nearly 50 years of professional ghost-hunting. He arrived home white and distraught and sat up most of the night writing a report of the incidents.

From his notes we can build up a precise picture of what is surely the most spectacular and baffling case of psychic phenomena yet experienced.

It was on December 8, 1937, that Harry Price first heard about Rosalie. A woman hearing him making a broadcast talk, telephoned him and told of a family seance held every Wednesday at her house when the spirit of a child always materialized. Price was invited to attend.

There were some conditions. Price had to promise never to reveal the identity of the sitters or the exact location. He was to bring no torch or light nor was he to speak or touch the materialization without permission.

He could, however, entirely control the room and the sitters up to the beginning of the seance and make any examinations he wished. Price accepted the terms and arranged to attend the session scheduled for December 15.

Room sealed

Rosalie was the daughter of a woman referred to throughout the incident as Mrs. Z. She was of French birth and had married a British army officer who had been killed in the first world war. The child, Rosalie, died of diphtheria in 1920.

In 1925, Mrs. Z. sensed the presence of her daughter during the night and heard her call: "Mother." After a time, Rosalie materialized and Mrs. Z. was able to clasp the hand of her little girl.

Later, friends suggested that regular seances should be held. It was to one of these that Harry Price had been invited.

Before sitting, he examined the sitting room in ruthless detail. He removed ornaments and the clock, locked the door, pocketed the key, and sealed the doors and windows with adhesive tape.

He covered the fireplace with sheets of paper and taped it in place, emptied every drawer, turned the settee upside down, examined the cushions, scrutinized every inch of the floorboards.

He opened the back of the radio set, and dusted starch powder around all movable objects, and in front of the door and chimney.

Mother sobbed

Eventually, when he was satisfied that the room was completely sealed from the outside world, the seance began.

A small lamp cast a glow over the six people seated in a circle. A few minutes after 10 P.M., as they sat in silence, Mrs. Z. began to sob.

Then she whispered: "Rosalie is here—don't speak," and Price sensed the presence of something close to him.

Through the gloom he could see the shape of a small girl, aged about six.

He asked whether he could touch the materialization, and permission was given. Price put out his hands and touched the arms of the girl.

Heart beating

He passed his hand over her face and body and found her flesh to be cooler than that of a normal human being.

Her hair, long and soft, fell about her shoulders. As he held her, Price could feel the child breathing. He lifted her right hand and felt her pulse which was beating at the rate of 90 a minute. He put his ear to Rosalie's chest and could clearly hear her heart beating. Price took both the child's hands in his own and turned her towards the light.

He saw what he later described as "a beautiful child which would have graced any nursery in the land." Her features were classical and her eyes bright and intelligent. Price then asked if he could question the child and this was agreed.

No explanation

To his first five questions about how she passed her time in the spirit world, no reply was received. But when he asked the child whether she loved her mother she replied in a low voice that she did. Mrs. Z. clasped Rosalie to her.

All the women were crying and Price recalled that he was also affected by the "touching and pathetic scene."

After five minutes, the apparition gradually faded and eventually disappeared. The lights were switched on and Price was asked to make any investigation he liked.

All his seals were intact and the powder was undisturbed. He toured the rest of the house, but could find no explanation for the phenomenon.

He never did, nor did the many other investigators who were intrigued by Price's account. Never again was any outsider allowed to see the child and Price honored his pledge of secrecy.

Harry Price died in 1948 leaving behind him a riddle destined to remain unsolved forever.

STILL UNSOLVED—THE SECRET OF THE RESTLESS DEAD

What mystery force broke the silence of this tomb?

As men stood in shocked silence, some unseen force could be heard ravaging the coffins in a family vault. Regularly avoiding the traps set, it invaded the privacy of the dead in a search for something which still remains a mystery.

THE MOON shimmered over the silver Caribbean and picked out the ornate coral and stone vault standing on a headland of the West Indian island of Barbados.

Suddenly, a procession of lantern-carrying men approached along the steep path leading to the tomb. A hundred yards away they stopped, transfixed as the sounds of crashing and splintering reverberated through the hot still night.

Deep in the earth, some indeterminate sinister force was wrecking the coffins of the dead. For years its handiwork had troubled and shocked the island. Now it had been caught red-handed in its act of pillage.

Leading the group of police and soldiers was the Governor, Field Marshal Viscount Combermere. Later he was to write: "I could sense no earthly thing was at work in the tomb. The night was hot, but all of us were shivering."

It was certain that no earthly thing was disturbing the dead in the vault of the Chase family. Soldiers with orders to kill guarded the tomb. The Governor himself had fixed seals on its lid. As the tomb was opened the noises ceased.

Restless dead

Wrenching open the vault the men found the coffins piled high in the center, the last one swaying as though spectral hands had just placed it there.

The story of the restless dead of Barbados has been probed by a dozen scientific investigations but no feasible explanation has ever been produced.

A routine funeral 80 years ago, provided a backdrop for the first act of the bizarre mystery.

On that hot July day, the body of the Honorable Thomas Chase, a well-to-do merchant and exporter, was carried up the steep path to the family's cliff-top vault.

Three members of the family were already interred there. As the mourners approached the grave, they were utterly unprepared for what was about to happen.

Guards posted

Six workmen moved forward with iron bars to prise up the heavy stone and reveal the five steps which lead down to the vault.

In his journal, the priest conducting the ceremony, the Rev. Thomas Orderson, described what happened next.

"The workmen who lifted the slab refused to carry Mr. Chase's body down into the vault. They appeared to be greatly agitated and were most adamant in their refusal to proceed further with the task at hand."

It was not surprising. The clergyman and mourners peered down into the gloom. The three coffins had been taken from their niches and thrown against the wall. One was broken.

The Barbados authorities were considerably disturbed over the incident. Had someone violated the grave in an attempt to rob the coffins? Guards were posted on the cliff top and required to inspect the seals on the Chase vault at least twice a day.

All in order

Nothing remarkable was seen; a daily inspection was continued, but the matter was largely forgotten.

Four years later, the authorities gathered at the same spot for another interment. A child of the family had died.

As the church service neared its end, three police officials hurried to the vault to examine the seals. Everything, it seemed, was in order. The vault, under guard for four years, showed no signs of tampering.

Inside, however, it was a different story. The bewildered officials found the coffins once again jumbled in the confines of the five by twelve foot vault.

Feeling roused

The lead-sheathed coffin of Thomas Chase, so heavy it required eight men to lift it, was on its side at the far end of the tomb.

Again the coffins were returned to their original positions and the entrance carefully sealed in the presence of witnesses.

A guard was placed within 50 feet of the vault with instructions to shoot anyone who approached it without authority.

But when the tomb was opened two months later, disarray once again was found.

By now public feeling was so aroused that Viscount Combermere decided to personally visit the tomb and lay a trap for the offenders.

Personal seals

Surveying the disorderly pile of coffins, the Governor ordered a sketch plan of their positions to be made. The vault was sounded and examined for concealed entrances and the floor covered with white sand, carefully brushed out smooth. The steps were sprinkled with wood ash, the slab cemented and chained in place, and the personal seals of the Governor and his aides placed on the tomb.

A few weeks later, a terrified sentry left his post to report rumblings and crashings coming from the tomb.

Summoned from his bed, Lord Combermere led a party of soldiers and police in lamp-lit procession to the vault.

Baffling fact

The seals were unbroken. The heavy stone slab was freed and slid back. The sand and ash remained undisturbed but the coffins were piled high in the center of the vault.

The last one, swaying as though it had hurriedly been placed there, toppled as they watched and fell with a crash to the floor.

Daylight revealed the most baffling fact of all. The coffins themselves had been reversed in position with their heads towards the door, something impossible to accomplish without taking the coffins outside to turn them round.

Thirty years ago, any chance of the mystery being solved

was cursorily brought to an end by the decision of the Chase family to remove the coffins to another cemetery in the hope that they might be left in peace.

Up to now they have. Whatever it was that broke the silence of the grave with the splinter and crash of timber has finally lost interest. Or so it is hoped.

WITNESS TO MURDER—BUT THE KILLER WAS A GHOST . . .

—and the crime was committed 300 years ago!

The film taken in a haunted mansion by Dr. Edward Morton would have rocked the world of psychic research back on its heels. But no one ever saw it. In a violent accident, the realm of the supernatural reached out to reclaim its secrets—and punish the mortal who had dared to snatch them.

THE DUSKY twilight of the summer evening took on a jagged and sinister brilliance, as the lanes outside an English Cotswolds village were bathed in the light of flames.

A fire-engine rumbled between the high hedges. Firemen ran forward with foam extinguishers. But it was too late. The car which lay on its side in the ditch was a knotted mass of red-hot steel and among the wreckage lay the body of a man.

He had been struggling to escape when the heat and the fumes had overcome him. Still gripped in his hand was a movie film canister. It was gaping open now and the flames had licked hungrily inside to devour the celluloid.

The world of the supernatural had, it seemed, reached out to reclaim its secrets and to punish the mortal who had dared to snatch them. For on the film which Dr. Edward Morton was taking to London for processing, was a ghostly murder.

The film, taken through infra-red lenses on the night of July 4, 1947, would have thrown the world of psychic research back on its heels. As it was, the man who took it was now dead, and the film a shriveled mass of ash.

Research needed

When Edward Morton, doctor of science, decided to organize a ghost hunt, everything was conducted with the clipped precision of a military operation.

He had a team of ten men, cameramen, technicians, recording engineers . . . experts of psychic phenomena.

A group of notetakers would record in duplicate everything that happened. Infra-red lenses would probe dusky corners, bringing the spotlight of science on to centuries of surmise and mystery.

For Dr. Morton was a realist. He believed that anything could be subjected to scientific examination with profitable results. It was just a question of painstaking research. If you went on carefully enough, long enough, you could get an answer—even to a haunting.

In the spring of 1947, Morton mounted the most impressive scientific examination of the supernatural ever devised.

He chose Potterdene Hall, a decaying mansion in England's picturesque Cotswolds for his tests. He got a good deal more than he bargained for.

Dying breath

Potterdene Hall was owned by an elderly industrialist who spent most of his time abroad. He wanted to sell the house and grounds and agreed that so long as no damage was caused, Morton could use the house for his experiments until some decision about its future was made.

The house was undoubtedly haunted. The ghostly occupants were said to include the "Wild Cavalier" who after a night of unsuccessful gambling had returned to Potterdene Hall and murdered his young wife.

With her dying breath, she had cursed him, and declared that his soul would haunt the hall for as long as a wall was left standing. The ghostly enactment of the murder had been witnessed many times.

· It seemed an ideal place for Dr. Morton's experiments. At the beginning of June, he moved in.

The hauntings were claimed to take place in a large ground floor room with french windows opening on to a terrace. It was here that Dr. Morton set up his equipment. A movie camera, tape recorder and a series of still cameras were mounted on easily maneuverable rubber-wheeled trolleys.

A routine

The team was split into threes and organized into eight-hour watches. Dr. Morton would have no regular watch but would be called whenever anything happened. ·

A series of cameras with trip wires would take care of any hoaxers. Soon the team had settled down to a regular routine. Two people on watch would be in the haunted room, the other patrolling the rest of the house. Dr. Morton had an office in an adjoining room.

For a month, nothing happened. Then in the first week of July, Frederick Redfearn, a professional psychic investigator attached to the party, said he sensed a change in the atmosphere. Something was about to happen.

The next night it did.

At 11 P.M., the microphones hung throughout the house began to feed sound into the loudspeakers in Morton's room. He switched on the tapes.

Sobbing girl

There were voices, laughter, the constant tapping of high heels, but the sounds had a strange unreality. A member of the team who was off duty and strolling near the lake, came in to report he had seen lights flashing in top floor windows.

Five other men, including Redfearn, were aroused and gathered among the equipment. At midnight, the temperature had dropped a startling five degrees.

Suddenly the figure of a man was seen in the corner of the room. Immediately the spools of the movie camera began to turn, and an automatic camera flashed off a series of high speed exposures.

The man was young and dark and clad in a costume of the mid-17th century. He strode by the researchers and through an open door into an adjoining room.

Swiftly they dragged the equipment through the entrance. Morton and Redfearn peered round the snout of the camera —and saw an incredible sight.

Avenging flames

On the floor of the room lay a blonde giirl, sobbing convulsively. Standing over her, a dagger running with blood, was the dark young man. The girl tried to rise, tried to clutch at the man's clothes, but he tore away.

The phenomenon was barely 20 feet away from the watchers. Despite the gloom, they could see the tragedy clearly. And the infra-red lens of the camera recorded it all.

The next day, in a state of high excitement, Dr. Morton departed with the film for London. They had developed a test section of the spool and found it to contain definite figures.

He never reached the process laboratories. In the early

evening avenging flames destroyed both him and his evidence. The still photographs which had remained at the hall were developed but were not conclusive.

The world of the occult, it seems, is jealous of its secrets. And if the fate of Dr. Morton is any guide it will protect them, if necessary, even with death.

DUEL TO THE DEATH—BEFORE A GHOST AUDIENCE

And the loser had died 50 years before!

For years there had been a hoodoo on London's Mohawk Theater; every play produced there had been a failure. But one night in 1929, the house was packed to watch a duel between two men. Only the scene had taken place 50 years before and the audience was composed of ghosts . . .

THE MOHAWK THEATER was full. The dress circle, pit, balcony, boxes and gallery were crowded to capacity with an audience settling eagerly in their seats, waiting for the curtain to rise.

They were happy and laughing, except for two men who sat in the front row of the stalls. On their faces, expressions of disbelief mingled with growing fear. Not surprisingly—it was 3:30 A.M., and the Mohawk Theater, in London's West End, had been derelict for five years.

The two men also knew without a shadow of doubt that apart from themselves the entire audience in the theater . . . was composed of ghosts!

This phenomenon, without equal in the annals of psychic research, took place over 30 years ago. Yet the reports of two experienced and independent observers who attended the phantom first night, remain on file, eerie, unexplained and classics of their kind.

They did not know until some time afterwards that they had witnessed a "second showing" of incidents which had happened at the Mohawk fifty years earlier, when two jealous men had faced each other on the stage—and one had crumpled lifeless into the footlights.

Researchers intrigued

For years the theater had had a jinx; no play produced there had much success and in 1929 it was closed while its owners decided what to do with it.

The next year it opened under another name and closed again in a few weeks. And throughout the years, whether opened or closed, ghosts were walking the Mohawk's boards.

In 1934, two psychic researchers, Maurice Rossington and Lewis Miller, intrigued by the legends surrounding the theater, decided to mount a proper investigation.

The management raised no objection to the probe, so long as the researchers did not let the press know, and kept the results of their investigations to themselves.

On December 5, 1934, Rossington and Miller moved into the Mohawk to spend the night there.

The place was uncomfortably lonely; there was an eerie and depressing stillness, unbroken except by creaking of woodwork and the occasional rattling of a window in the wind.

Saw the girl

After wandering up and down staircases and patrolling corridors and ante-rooms, the men went backstage. Dust lay thick on the boards; there were signs of long neglect everywhere.

Miller heard a movement in the property room. Cautiously opening the door, he looked in. He saw a man, bending down, and handling a stage sword. Miller took a step forward and the man vanished.

Meanwhile, on the stage, Rossington suddenly had the feeling someone was watching him. He turned—and saw the girl.

Peering anxiously from the wings was a tall slender woman with dark hair and eyes. The pallor of her face was startlingly white. As he watched, she glided noiselessly across the stage, and disappeared into the opposite wing.

The men, both jolted by their experiences, moved together into the stalls and sat down near the orchestra rail, to make notes of the happenings. Suddenly they heard voices, laughter and bustle.

Turning round, they saw to their amazement that they were not alone: all the seats were occupied by people wearing the costume of fifty years earlier.

Clash of weapons

The house was full, but the people did not seem real. They had a deathlike pallor. Seated alone in the box was the woman Rossington had seen on the stage.

Both men now saw her, and both, in independent reports, described exactly what she wore and how she looked.

She no longer wore a cloak but was in a rich evening dress. She was leaning forward gazing fixedly at the stage.

The noise ceased abruptly as the curtain rose revealing a woodland scene. A duel with rapiers was about to take place between two men, a tall fair-haired man with a beard and a dark clean-shaven one. Suddenly they began to fight.

There was silence in the auditorium, broken only by the clash of weapons. Miller glanced at the woman in the box.

She was watching the duellists, following every thrust and guard with intense anxiety and excitement.

Suddenly the fair man lunged with lightning rapidity and pierced his adversary in the chest. He gave a gasping cry, staggered and fell. There was a cry from the woman in the box—but of pleasure, not pain. She clapped her hands exultantly.

Stories tallied

The curtain fell and the auditorium was once again empty and in darkness.

The next day Rossington and Miller began their reports. They did them in separate rooms. Each man wrote down exactly what he had seen; the stories were similar in every detail.

Then they started research into the Mohawk's history and uncovered an uncanny coincidence.

In 1880, the theater had staged a play called "The Watching Eye." In it were two leading actors, Guy Lang and Raymond Ross. Ross was known to be very much in love with Mrs. Lang.

In the play there was a duel between Ross and Lang, and one night Ross killed Lang. The stage foils always had buttons on their points to prevent their wounding anyone, but on this occasion the foil Ross used had lost its button.

Faces familiar

Rumor had it that Mrs. Lang had bribed the property man to remove the button, but there was no direct evidence of this.

From that time onward, the theater was said to be haunted and no play ever succeeded. In fact, two years after the

114

researchers visited it, the building was demolished to make way for an office block.

There is a footnote to the story. Shortly before his death in 1945, Maurice Rossington was delving into the theatrical archives of a newspaper.

He came across two faded photographs which seemed familiar. Then in a flash he recognized the faces of the opponents in the fatal duel.

Rossington turned over the pictures and read the names— Guy Lang and Raymond Ross . . .

SCREAMS OF DEATH FORETOLD BOY'S DOOM

And only the victim failed to hear them

For centuries, an impending death in the Carnsen family had always been signified by a series of piercing, blood-chilling screams. Everyone heard them—except the person doomed to die. They rang out again when 10-year-old John Carnsen lay sick, despite the doctor's assurance that he would recover. . . .

THE TWO doctors turned away from the bedside of young John Carnsen and stooped to pack away their instruments. "He is on the mend," the younger man told John Carnsen's mother.

Yet there was no joy, or even relief, in the room. For everyone knew that ten-year-old John Carnsen was going to die. Early that morning—on June 5, 1901—the omens of doom had gathered around Flesbury, a remote English mansion near Bude in Cornwall.

For centuries, an impending death in the Carnsen family

had been signified in a highly individualistic and blood-chilling way. In the early morning piercing screams would rack the house, heard by everyone but the person doomed to die.

And early on that Friday morning the screams had echoed again through the corridors of Flesbury. Only John Carnsen had not heard them.

He had been taken ill in the spring of 1901 and for many weeks his life hung in the balance. Then at the end of May he began to rally, then to recover.

They waited

Soon he was getting out of bed for a few hours a day and sitting by the window of his first·floor room in the west wing.

The Carnsens had two other children, Mary, 14, and Michael, aged seven. They spent a good deal of time with their brother. They too had heard the screams but were warned to say nothing about them.

Now Flesbury was waiting with fatalistic resignation for the boy to die.

The screams had not been heard for ten years. Then, William Carnsen, John's grandfather, lay dying in a darkened room on the ground floor. Two years before that, they had rung out, and servants had found his wife dead in a chair in the drawing room.

Now Marcus Carnsen, John's father, was master of Flesbury. He had never personally heard the screams of death before and was highly cynical of them. He still believed, despite the wealth of tradition, that there was a rational solution.

"What's the matter?"

It had been 7 A.M. on June 5, that the first shriek rang out. Mary and Michael sleeping in a room on the second floor awoke with horror.

A minute later, the door opened and Marcus Carnsen came in. "What is the matter?" he asked. "Who is screaming in that dreadful manner?"

"Papa," answered Michael, "we don't know. It wasn't one of us, but it seemed quite close."

"Go down to the kitchen, Mary," the father said. "See if something has happened down there."

The girl went down and found the housekeeper standing alone.

She declared she had heard the shrieks and was about to go into the scullery to see if anything had happened there.

Heard nothing

The two housemaids and pantry boy had also heard the commotion. The screams came, they said, from a long way off. When Mary returned upstairs she found her father talking to the doctors who had just arrived.

They too had heard a female voice as they had walked up the drive towards the house. Mary then ran upstairs to John's room. Had he suffered some kind of fit?

Anxiously she threw open the door—and found her brother lying peacefully in bed. Their mother was sitting by the window reading a magazine.

Nothing could have been quieter and more composed than the room and its inmates. "Johnny, how quiet you look," said the girl. "Have you been asleep?"

"No," he replied. "I heard the doctors come up the drive." Obviously he had heard no noise of an unusual kind.

Gurgling sound

The doctors were now on their way up, and Mary, as she left, beckoned her mother to follow. She told her of the screams. Her mother went pale and began to tremble.

Marcus Carnsen, determined to get to the root of the matter, ordered an immediate search of the house and grounds. But nothing was found. He questioned the housekeeper and the bailiff.

One point soon became clear: the shrieks had come from *inside* the house. The stories of all those who heard them tallied: there had been three screams at short intervals.

It was as though a woman's voice was being strained to the utmost. Then the scream had ended in a rattling gurgling sound.

What was utterly inexplicable was that the shrieks were loudest on the staircase in the west wing and should therefore have been almost deafening in John's room. Yet no one in there had heard a sound . . .

Nothing more could be done. The servants were given strict orders not to allow any report of what had happened to leak out. Then everyone waited . . . and prayed.

Last breath

The doctors visited regularly and pronounced continued improvement. John got up, and was even allowed downstairs. Could it be that the screams of death had held an empty threat?

Then a week later, he took a sudden, fatal, and completely inexplicable turn for the worse. Three weeks to the day from when the shrieks were heard, he slipped into a coma.

At midnight, just before the end, those who waited in his room again heard sounds of wailing and lamentation passing through the house. Then the noise ceased. John Carnsen had drawn his last breath.

The shrieks have been heard twice since in the corridors of Flesbury: on the deaths of Marcus Carnsen and his wife.

Since then, the house has been little used as a family residence. But the mystery is no nearer a solution. Doubtless the eerie sounds will return the next time death comes to Flesbury.

SAVED FROM THE SEA BY A PHANTOM CREW

They snatched him from drowning—then vanished!

Loaded to capacity, the lifeboats moved away from the sinking ship leaving William Schindler alone in the Indian Ocean. Finally, another lifeboat found him and 15 pairs of hands hauled him to safety. But, uncannily, when he reached land, he was the only occupant—and the boat's supplies were untouched.

THE SUN swept pitilessly over the Indian Ocean and flickered across the aimless floating wreckage which had once been the Dutch freighter *John de Kruif*. A few bodies drifted by, still supported by their orange life jackets. But they were dead.

Clinging to a large wooden spar, William Schindler looked round the sweep of ocean and could see no other living thing.

The torrid violence of a few hours earlier when the freighter had been battered under the waves by Japanese bombers had dissolved into a surrealistic calm.

It was midday on March 7, 1942, and William Schindler was reconciling himself to death. But it was not to be. Instead he was to become the central figure in an uncanny, completely inexplicable, drama.

Two days later he was found, suffering from exposure but alive, in the bottom of a drifting lifeboat.

Time to leave

He claimed that it had contained at least 15 men and women. They had lifted him in to safety.

Yet when found he was the only occupant, the boat's oars and sails were still stowed and the emergency supplies still untouched!

Early in March, 1942, Schindler was an American press syndicate correspondent reporting the Japanese conquest of Java. Batavia had just fallen. Soon the whole island would be in enemy hands: it was time to get out.

Schindler boarded the *John de Kruif*, a Dutch vessel bound for India. Also aboard were the last Dutch officers to leave, as well as oil company executives and their wives—240 people in all.

About 200 miles off the coast, the ship was overtaken by Japanese aircraft. Relentlessly the bombs began to fall. By 10 A.M. the ship had slewed over on its side and disappeared.

Turned away

The water was full of people . . . people swimming, screaming, and drowning. Among the debris, Schindler could see a lifeboat—the only one in sight—loaded to capacity and moving slowly away from the disaster scene.

Schindler swam as fast as he could towards the boat. It was crowded with bedraggled bodies. A few sailors and officers were rowing stolidly. Schindler put on a spurt and reached the side of the lifeboat. He shouted and lifted his arms ready to be rescued.

But no one reached down to save him. The people in the boat only stared and turned away. He pleaded with the man at the tiller: "Give me a break—I can't swim to Java!"

The helmsman shook his head: "We're full," he told Schindler. Wildly the man in the water grabbed for an oar but it was tilted out of his reach. He snatched at a rope trailing from the stern but someone in the boat jerked it from his fingertips.

The boat moved away and Schindler was alone. Now exhaustion was pulling at his arms and legs like a dead weight, dragging down his whole body. No longer was the air hideous with screams: he could see no other swimmers.

How long?

Fighting away panic he lay back in his lifejacket. One moment he was deep in the trough of a wave, the next riding high on a crest.

He wondered how long it would be before he drowned; he knew that eventually his neck would become tired and his face would droop into the water.

He remembered a story he had heard about a man who had drowned: this man had become so tired and dazed that he forgot which was sea and which was sky; which was water and which was air, and which to breathe for life.

How long, thought Schindler, will it be before I forget?

A large wooden spar drifted by and he clasped his arms around it. He wondered what time it was. The sun was pretty far over to the west; must be late afternoon.

No-one noticed

Suddenly he saw a little spike sticking up over the horizon. At first he thought it was a submarine periscope, then as he was lifted by another wave, he saw it was the mast of a lifeboat.

The boat was not moving much. He knew, weak as he was, that he could make it if the vessel continued to drift towards him. He swam frantically, but no one seemed to have noticed him: the oars hung motionless from the sides of the boat.

Schindler reached the side of the vessel, gasping and clutching onto the steep steel sides but they were too high for him to climb unaided.

Suddenly two men leaned over the side of the boat, grasped him and hauled him up. As he fell into the craft his hand caught a small medallion worn by one of his rescuers and jerked it off.

Dreamless sleep

There were at least fifteen people in the boat. A woman helped him to lie comfortably on the floorboards.

Then he heard the sound of oars swinging in long steady sweeps, driving the boat towards safety. He fell into a deep dreamless sleep.

On the morning of March 9, the American frigate *Makepeace* sighted a white-painted lifeboat drifting among patches of weed 400 miles off the Java coast.

It bore the name of *John de Kruif*. The oars and sails were still stowed, the emergency stores untouched. In the bottom of the boat was the huddled figure of William Schindler.

When he eventually told his story no one believed him. In his delirium, they said that he must have struggled into the boat. In vain he said that the sides were too high for any man—particularly one in his fatigued condition—to scale unaided.

They probably would have given his tale never a second thought if they hadn't found a tiny gold medallion clasped firmly in his right hand . . .

THE TRAIN THAT DROVE ITSELF

—after the driver had died on the footplate . . .

For 15 miles, the early-morning commuter train threaded its way along one of Belgium's busiest rail routes, obeying signals, stopping at stations. Yet, all the time, the driver was slumped lifeless at the controls. Railway experts spent weeks examining the equipment; at the end, they could offer no rational explanation.

ON THE MORNING of September 3, 1950 a four-car electric commuter special left Antwerp's Central Station for the 15 mile run to Brussels.

The train was crowded—as it always was. Yet on this morning, the hundreds of office workers and businessmen who packed the carriages were going on a journey they would remember all their lives.

For on this occasion the 8:10 from Antwerp had a dead man at the controls. The half-hour journey was along one of Belgium's busiest rail routes, littered with signals and point junctions.

All these, the train had negotiated safely . . . while Gaston Meyers, its 30-year-old driver, slumped lifeless over the controls.

The train had no automatic control gear; everything had to be done by the driver. Railway experts spent weeks examining the locomotive's equipment.

Sleepless night

Eventually, came their conclusions: "There appears to us to be no technical explanation for what occurred on the 8:10 train. We are at a loss to put forward any rational reason for the incident."

And there, for 15 years, the mystery has remained.

The saga of the train that drove itself began at 6:30 A.M. on September 3 when Gaston Meyers reported for duty at the Antwerp Motive Power Depot. He looked pale and feverish.

He told workmates that he had spent a sleepless night and was running a high temperature. Against the family's advice he had come to work.

The Operating Superintendent spoke to Meyers and advised him to see the depot doctor. Meyers refused, saying that he would be all right.

After a cup of coffee and a rest, he certainly did look a little better. At 7:45, he entered the one-man cabin of his train and took it out of the engine sheds and into the station.

Normal trip

Through the intercom he told his guard, 41-year-old Jacques Lynden, that he felt "a little hazy" but was quite well enough to continue.

The train left Antwerp one minute late. As the signal lights changed, it drew away from Number Five platform and went through a series of points onto the main line to Brussels.

Six minutes ahead was a similar commuter train, and four minutes behind would be another: strict adherence to schedules was therefore vital.

In the first compartment of the leading carriage, Paul

Harmel, an executive in a textile importing firm, was reading his morning newspaper.

He recalled later that about five minutes after leaving Antwerp the train slowed rather suddenly and then accelerated. Apart from this the journey was quite normal.

The 8:10 rattled through the suburbs and, obeying a warning signal, began to slow down for the first station—Blancefloer, on the fringe of a residential estate.

Warning blast

An official on the platform recalled that the train came in smoothly and stopped in the required position. He did not notice who the driver was as the train moved past—his head was down and he seemed to be concerned with something on the instrument panel in front of him.

A minute later, the train moved off and station staff prepared to receive the following one.

In the guard's van, Jacques Lynden glanced at his newspaper and kept routine observation. A few minutes after leaving Antwerp, he had spoken to Meyers over the intercom and the driver had said that he felt much better.

Now Lynden settled down to a normal, rather boring, spell of duty. As the train picked up speed from Blancefloer, he heard the hooter sound a warning blast.

He glanced from his observation window to see work progressing on a parallel set of tracks. The platelayers moved back as the train went past.

Then it halted at several other stations. No one noticed anything strange.

Something strange

In his signal cabin some miles down the line, Maurice Tancre set points and signals to receive the 8:10 from Antwerp. He noted from his indicator board that the train was slowing for a warning signal as it entered his section.

As the train passed his box, Tancre glanced down into the driving cab. Then he froze: he could see no one at the controls.

Tancre hurried to his phone and called the next box along the line. "There's something strange about the 8:10," he reported. "I could not see the driver."

The next man set a slow-down signal and watched intently as the approaching train obeyed and passed his box at a crawl. He too was amazed to see the control cabin apparently empty.

The train was now approaching Vermeylen—the last station before Brussels. The signalman's call to central control had been passed on to the Vermeylen stationmaster asking him to check with the 8:10 driver that everything was all right.

Stationmaster Leon Vreven ordered a stop signal to halt the train and walked down the platform to the driver's cabin. Sure enough, no one was visible through the side windows.

He was dead

He jerked open the door. Lying over the control panel, his hands dangling towards the floor, was Gaston Meyers. Vreven knew at once that he was dead.

The doctor who hurried to the scene expecting to find a victim of some kind of heart attack, found instead something far more mysterious.

"This man," he said, "has been dead for at least half an hour." In vain, station staff insisted that the train had been in Vermeylen barely five minutes. A post mortem confirmed the doctor's view.

There is no rational explanation for the phenomenon. Reluctantly, we must conclude that no human hand guided the 8:10 from Antwerp to Brussels that fateful morning.

For what other solution can there be?

HIS CALLING CARD WAS THE ACE OF SPADES . . .

Mystery figure brought death to the card table . . .

Death came to the tense atmosphere of the high-stake gambling table to claim the life of a cheating card-sharper. It came in the bizarre form of a tall man in a black cloak, who, before two witnesses, snatched the victim through a window and out into the night.

THE FANS turned slowly, but the air, stifling and sluggish, hardly moved. Malta in August, thought Lieutenant Charles Danvers, was no place for a British officer to be.

The night of August 3, 1935, was the hottest of a sweltering summer. Lieutenant Danvers sat at the window of his quarters in the garrison on the Verdala side of the Grand Harbor and looked down through the eucalyptus trees to where the lights of the port twinkled and danced and the steamship generators hummed and vibrated.

Across the barrack square, Danvers could see the lights of the Mess and hear sporadic conversation, an occasional burst of laughter. Another mammoth card session was under way.

There was plenty of time for cards in the British garrison in Malta between the wars. Boredom was their constant enemy. They drove it off with parties, guest nights, sporting events, but the tedium soon returned. Gambling, it seemed, was the only pleasure to last, and that was thanks to Humphrey Saunders.

But on the night of August 3, Humphrey Saunders was going to banish Malta's bored lethargy for some time to come. He was going to die—in a macabre, horrific, and totally mysterious manner.

Well-known figure

What brought Saunders to the island was something no one knew much about. He was said to have served in the Indian Army and subsequently joined a number of British ex-officers who joined the Austrian cavalry after the first World War.

He did not stay long in Vienna and by the time Lieutenant Danvers was posted to Malta, Saunders was a well-known character among the English residents and garrison.

As he was an ex-officer he was made an honorary member of the Mess and could be found there several evenings a week playing billiards, snooker, or more likely, sitting in at the card table.

At cards he appeared unbeatable: indeed he was said to live on his winnings, and there was no shortage of officers who fancied their hand at whist, poker or *ecarte*, happy to give him a game.

It was rumored that he cheated, but no one could prove it.

High stakes

On the night of August 3, Saunders had dined with the regiment. Afterwards he had adjourned to the mess and sat down with half a dozen subalterns to play *vingt-et-un*. The stakes were high and the tension soon rose as Saunders repeatedly dealt himself favorable cards.

Lieutenant Danvers did not play. He stood by the window, watched a couple of hands and then went to his quarters intending to write some letters. The night was so hot he could not concentrate.

He lit a cigar and sat by his window.

It had been a guest night: the regimental band had been playing on a space outside the windows of the officer's mess. They had finished now, but there were still a few people about.

The open windows of the mess were still aglow. A clock struck 11 P.M. Glancing again across the square, Danvers reached up to close the shutters of his room.

Voices raised

Then he paused. Across the square he could see a remarkably tall man in a long dark cloak standing motionless under one of the mess windows.

Something about the appearance of this solitary, shrouded figure attracted his attention. To be wearing such clothes in a Mediterranean heatwave seemed peculiar. Who could he be? What was he waiting for?

Danvers has recalled: "I became aware of a kind of chill and numbness creeping through me. I felt a foreboding of impending evil. As I watched the motionless figure I was aware of raised voices coming from the Mess.

"I recognized Saunders' voice shouting: 'I tell you I dealt myself the ace of spaces!' There was further tumult."

With a leap, the cloaked man sprang on to the window sill and disappeared through the curtains into the Mess. Danvers was unable to see anything further.

Scattered cards

Then after a few seconds, an ear-piercing scream rang out—a harsh appalling cry of rage and terror, and to his horror and utter amazement, Danvers saw the man in the cloak reappear at the window with Saunders gripped in his arms. Both men vanished around the corner of the building.

Danvers clutched at his telephone and called out the guard. Telling the sergeant of the guard to search the enclosure for two men fighting, the lieutenant ran into the Mess.

In the card-room he found chaos. A whist table was overturned and cards scattered across the room. On the floor, surrounded by half a dozen officers, lay Saunders. He was dead.

A formal military inquiry revealed that no civilian was in the garrison after 10 P.M.

The card players gave evidence that after a dispute over the dealing of an ace, a momentary gust of air seemed to shake the nearest window-sash.

Simultaneously, the card table was stirred—and Saunders, throwing up his hands, slumped in his chair gasping as though in a fit.

Classic mystery

Medical evidence was that he had died of a heart attack. No one else had seen the cloaked man, and Danvers began to wonder whether he had imagined the scene.

Then, a week later, he was talking to a fellow officer, occupier of the quarters above his own, who on the evening of August 3, had been lying, sick with "Malta fever," on a bed near the window.

The officer, Captain Roger Atkinson, brought the subject up: "I fear I must have been delirious on that night," he said. "I could swear I saw a tall man in a long cloak jump through a window in the Mess . . ."

Danvers said nothing about his experience until his retirement from the army years later. No psychic researchers he consulted could offer any explanation. Nor has anyone.

After nearly 30 years, the case of the Man in the Black

Cloak stands alone as a bizarre and classic mystery of the unknown.

THE MAN THEY COULDN'T HANG

Sentenced to death—but he dreamed he would live!

Three times the hangman tried to execute John Lee, sentenced to death for the murder of his employer. And each time, the trapdoors of the gallows inexplicably failed to work. Only Lee himself remained calm; he had always maintained his innocence—and he had dreamed that he would not be hanged.

JOHN LEE WAS only 20. His thin white shirt and narrow black trousers revealed the frailty of his body. He walked along the corridors of Exeter Prison on the morning of February 23, 1885, with his head held high and his face impassive.

It was hardly the face of a man going to the gallows. Yet John Lee was not an ordinary man.

He was to become known as "the man they couldn't hang" . . . the only condemned murderer in the annals of crime who has stood on the scaffold with the noose around his neck—and lived to tell the tale.

The story of John Lee has become a macabre and inexplicable classic.

For Lee *knew* he was not going to die: he dreamed the night before the execution that the trap would fail to drop . . . in exactly the way that it actually happened!

131

No mercy

Lee had for the previous three years been employed by an elderly spinster, Miss Emma Anne Whitehead Keyes, at her house on Britain's Devon coast as gardener and general handyman.

He received four shillings a week from his wealthy and austere employer.

On the night of November 14, 1884, Miss Keyes was found dead in the pantry. Her head had been gashed and pulped by a hatchet, and her throat cut by a garden knife Lee had been using.

John Lee, who slept in a cubbyhole adjoining the pantry, was arrested and charged with murder.

The evidence at the trial, held in Exeter on January 4, was purely circumstantial but conclusive. Lee was sentenced to death, and the jury made no recommendation for mercy.

Trivial offence

The prosecution's case rested on the harsh regime Miss Keyes imposed on her servants. She worked Lee and the other servants hard and for long hours, restricted their food and paid them the lowest possible wages.

Particularly did she victimize John Lee. Small though his wages were, she twice reduced them for some trivial offence or insubordination. The last reduction was of a shilling a week.

The prosecution played up this last wage cut as the last straw.

Yet in court, Lee stayed strangely calm and impassive. He did not look like a man who would kill in a sudden spasm of rage.

Asking Lee if he had anything to say, the judge commented on his even bearing. Lee replied: "The reason, my lord, that I am so calm and collected is that I will not be hanged. The Lord knows that I am innocent."

As John Lee slept through what was expected to be his last night on earth, the executioner tested the scaffold.

Tested five times

The drop consisted of two doors secured underneath by a bolt. The prisoner would stand with a foot on each door, and when the bolt was withdrawn, the doors would naturally fall apart.

The drop was tested five times, and on every occasion worked perfectly.

At 7 A.M. on the morning of February 23, Lee awoke and told a warder of a dream he had had. "I dreamed," he told Warder Samuel Bennett, "that I was being led through a small garden and was mounted upon a scaffold with a hood over my head and a rope around my neck.

"I heard the hangman pull the lever and felt the bolt withdrawn beneath my feet, but the trap failed to drop. I feel sure that I will not be hanged."

Less than half an hour later, his dream came true. . . .

The scaffold had been erected in a small garden within the prison walls well out of sight of Lee's cell. In fact, Lee did not even know there was a garden within the prison.

Lever pulled

At 8 A.M., he left his cell for the walk to the gallows. His feet were strapped together, a hood was slipped over his head and the noose adjusted.

The lever was pulled, there was the sharp click of the bolt being withdrawn, but Lee did not disappear through the trapdoor, for the doors failed to open.

The hangman, prison officials and witnesses stood silent and open-mouthed. But Lee neither spoke nor made any movement: he was the calmest man in the prison yard.

Lee was moved from the trapdoor, and immediately the doors fell open.

The condemned man was returned to his cell while officials tested the drop. Every time, it worked smoothly and perfectly.

Again Lee took his place. Again the lever was pulled. Again nothing happened.

Chaplain wept

It was set yet again, and Lee placed upon it. For the third time, the bolt was withdrawn and nothing happened. The executioner and the guards stamped on the trap, but still nothing happened.

Now, for the first time in that dreadful half-hour, Lee spoke. The hood billowed slightly as he said: "I shall not be hanged. The Lord knows I am innocent."

The Chaplain, tears streaming down his face, interrupted to plead: "It is God's intervention. You must not try further to hang this boy."

The Governor ordered Lee back to his cell. A special report was rushed to the Home Secretary in London. Eventually the boy's sentence was commuted to life imprisonment.

Lee spent 20 years in jail. He lived a further 15 years after his release and died in 1920.

John Lee would never speak about his ordeal at the scaffold. All he would say was: "I was innocent. I knew I wouldn't die."

THE CHAMPION NAMED THE DAY HE WOULD DIE ...

And the omens of doom came tragically true ...

Alberto Ascari knew to the day, almost to the minute, when he would die. Twenty years earlier his father had died at the wheel of a racing car. Ascari knew his own death was to be a "carbon copy" of his father's—and he was powerless to prevent it.

THE LAST LAP of the World Grand Prix Drivers' Championship began as autumn tinged the leaves of the Royal Park on the outskirts of Milan.

It was the first week of September 1955 and the standard-bearers carrying the banners of competing nations marched out on to the white concrete of the Monza racetrack.

Alberto Ascari, sitting in the Ferrari pits, watched the sun climb over the hills. The sky was china-blue and a breeze whispered through the sycamores.

Yet Ascari, world champion of the two previous years, and regarded by many as the fastest of all racing drivers, looked at the beauty around him and saw only the promise of death . . his own.

He had known for years the day death would come for him, and this was the day: the eighth of September, 1955, when the sun was shining, the sky was blue, and the Italian Grand Prix was soon to be held.

STRANGE DESTINIES

A blue sky

It is an unimaginative driver who, when negotiating that final Monza bend—the Vialone—sometimes during a race, does not remember the tragic fate of Alberto Ascari who died there at a time and in circumstances which he himself had forecast to the last detail.

This was the date 20 years earlier when his father, Antonio Ascari, had died at the wheel of an Alfa Romeo during the Italian Grand Prix.

Alberto, a great believer in the omens of numerology—the Italians call it "Cabela"—was convinced that he would follow his father's footsteps, even to the grave. And never before had the omens been so persistently strong.

He was 36, the age at which his father had died. Antonio had crashed four days before his fatal pile-up. Alberto, driving a Lancia, had been pulled from Monte Carlo Harbor four days earlier when his car had plunged off the road in a race at Monaco.

Antonio had died beneath a clear blue sky, swerving to avoid a cat which ran into his wheels. The sky today was clear and blue.

A bad knock

Ascari shivered in the sharp morning. His tutor and friend, ex-champion Luigi Villoresi, thumped him on the shoulder. "Forget it, Alberto," he said. "The good drivers stay alive. The bad ones buy it. The stars and the numbers have no more meaning than the tales of old wives."

Ascari smiled. "I can't win, can I?" he said. "If I'm right, I'll never know."

He went over to his flame-red Ferrari which mechanics had pushed out from the pits into the sunlight.

"Why do you need to practice again?" Villoresi asked. "You took a bad knock at Monaco. Why not rest until the race?"

An early lunch

But Ascari said he had to reassure himself once again that his nerve had not been shattered. "If I wait too long, I'll spend the rest of my life at half-throttle," he explained.

Despite Villoresi's earnest advice, Ascari beckoned the mechanics to ready the car for a practice run.

They had an early lunch with fellow-drivers Eugenio Castellotti and Count Johnny Lurani. The gay Castellotti, sensing Ascari's somber mood, tried to distract him, and gradually Alberto began to relax.

There were several hours before the race; the bell went for final practice. Ascari got up from the table.

"Take it easy," said Villoresi. Ascari patted his shoulder. "I will," he said. "This is just a few laps to keep in training."

A silence

The sleek Ferrari bellowed powerfully as it moved slowly through the paddock on its way to the track. Ascari was wearing all his lucky charms, his blue sweater and his famous blue motor-cycling helmet.

As the car turned on to the white concrete, Villoresi came over for a last word. "Just take it easy," he repeated.

Ascari smiled. "It's growing cold," he said. They were the last words he ever spoke. He began his practice run as smoothly as ever and went through two laps in classic style. He overtook a Maserati and another works Ferrari.

On the third lap he began unexpectedly to speed up and disappeared down a tree-lined section of the course.

His friends watched him sweep through several fast turns,

roar through a tunnel along a straight and through two gentle right-handers up to the Vialone bend.

Suddenly, ominously, the noise of the exhaust cut out. There was a silence, more nerve-wracking than any racing-car bellow.

A black cat

His friends began to run, but they were already too late. The Ferrari had come to grief at a corner Ascari would normally have taken flat out without a tremor. Something had happened to cause the car to fishtail at high speed.

The fishtail became a spin. The machine turned over and skidded off the course upside down. They found Ascari lying terribly injured beside the car. He was just alive.

Castellotti saw a black cat slinking off into the woods. Had this been the harbinger of doom?

Seconds later Alberto Ascari died in Villoresi's arms. Death, the unwanted companion, had visited at last. Ascari had died in the manner and on the day that he knew he would.

And Luigi Villoresi, looking up, saw the sun was still shining, and the sky was still a pale china blue.

A VOICE FROM THE GRAVE—THIRTY YEARS AFTER

Vicar heard the cries of a man he had buried . . .

A voice cried desperately for help from the darkness of a country churchyard—and a terrible story unfolded. The cries were those of a man the village priest had buried years before. And a death-bed confession revealed that he had gone to his grave while still alive.

THE REVEREND PETER POTTER sat by his friends in the country vicarage preparing his sermon. Autumn twilight was falling, and mist rose damply on the hills which ringed the Warwickshire village of Breek in England's Midlands.

Suddenly there was a tap on the window. The elderly priest looked up, and froze. Pressed against the window-pane was a ghastly white face.

The lips were moving as if the owner was trying to say something. There was a frantic appealing look in the pale wide open eyes. Then Potter heard a desperate and doleful cry: "Let me out . . . let me out."

He knew the face and the voice. They belonged to a man Potter had buried over twenty years ago.

It was only a week later, on October 8, 1931, that the priest heard the terrible sequel to the incident. In a death-bed confession, the retired village doctor admitted that the man Potter had buried had not been dead . . . only deeply drugged.

And ever since, the churchyard had been haunted by the stifled cries of the man buried alive.

Pretty widow

The story began in 1911, when Potter first came to the village. Apart from a retired doctor we can call Jenkins, there were few people with whom Potter had anything in common. His life outside the church was rather lonely.

But the vicarage pleased him. It was old, picturesque, but not too large for one person, a housekeeper and a maid.

He had only been in the village a short time when he was called upon to officiate at the funeral of Charles Pratt, an elderly corn-broker, who left a young and pretty widow.

It was a routine burial and Potter had no reason to connect it with the events which followed.

"Let me out"

A short time later, the vicar, who had been spending the day with friends some miles away, returned home late. He was crossing the churchyard when he heard a voice cry: "Let me out . . . let me out."

The cries seemed to come from a group of graves close to the path on which he was walking.

It was a dark close night and very still. "Who are you?" asked Potter. There was no reply. Then the cries began again. Thinking that someone was trying to frighten him, he searched the churchyard, stick in hand. There was no living person there.

He hurried to the house, sensing all the while that he was being followed.

A few nights later, the same thing occurred. He was crossing the churchyard when he again heard the cries. Again he searched, and could find no one.

A confession

The years went by, the cries were heard spasmodically, and the vicar became accustomed to them. Then, on that October evening in 1931, the terrifying manifestation appeared at his window, and the Reverend Potter wondered how much more he could stand.

The following week Dr. Jenkins, gravely ill, sent for the vicar.

"I haven't many more hours to live," the old man said, "and I shall not rest in my grave unless I confess to you something very dreadful I did many years ago.

"The memory of it has been a torment to me. I am truly

140

penitent. Will you promise to regard what I say as strictly confidential until after my death?"

The priest agreed. Then Dr. Jenkins told his story.

Strange idea

Over thirty years ago, village gossip had it that the young Mrs. Pratt was having an affair with some unknown man. Pratt heard the rumors and resolved to put his suspicions to the test.

He conceived the strange idea of pretending to be dead, to see how his supposed sudden demise would affect his wife. He took his friend Dr. Jenkins into his confidence, and asked his assistance.

Eventually, the doctor consented to help him. He had his reasons for doing so: for it was he who had been meeting Mrs. Pratt clandestinely, and he wished to marry her.

He told Pratt he would give him a mild opiate which would last just long enough to show to what degree if any, his wife had been affected by his fake demise.

Instead of giving Pratt a mild drug, Jenkins gave him a very strong one, promptly wrote out a death certificate, informed the authorities, and got in touch with the local undertaker!

Constant torment

The still unconscious Pratt was placed in his coffin and buried the next day by Potter. One of the men who carried the coffin to the churchyard said afterwards that he heard a movement inside it, but was told it was just his fancy.

Within a few months of the premature burial, Jenkins married Mrs. Pratt. It brought him little happiness. They quarreled continually, separated, and the wife died aged 41.

As for Jenkins, he dreaded passing the churchyard after

dark and was constantly tormented by mental visions of Pratt enduring the dreadful agony of his premature interment.

Dr. Jenkins died within a few hours of his confession. Potter gave a full statement to the police in Warwick, but there seemed no grounds for proceedings; all the culprits were now dead.

With the death of Dr. Jenkins, the haunting of Breek churchyard ceased. The spine-chilling cries were never heard again.

DIVE TO DEATH—WITH A GHOST AT THE CONTROLS

And an hour later it happened again!

Deliberately, it seemed, Johnny Holmes crashed in flames amid the Battle of the Marne. Almost immediately, two of his friends took off from the makeshift airfield. Within minutes, both had crashed. And both reported that Holmes had wrenched the controls away from them.

THE Battle of the Marne was reaching its grisly climax in September 1914 and the leaves were shaken early from the trees by the continual roar of explosive and the pounding of bombs into the earth.

Day and night the fire of battle glowed in the sky, flickering in the flimsy canvas and wiring of the few aeroplanes which, for the first time, were participating in a war.

From makeshift airfields a few miles behind the front they spluttered into the sky to fire their puny guns and do sporadic reconnaissance. There were aircraft of the Royal Air

142

Flying Corps and of the Australian Flying Corps. Both were manned by young men of from 19 to 24. They were wild both in the air and on the ground. They were impulsive and fearless. Nothing, it seemed, could shake them.

Fatal spins

Nothing, until the morning of September 17, 1914, when the specter of a young pilot wrenched the controls from the hands of two airmen and sent them spinning dizzily and fatally to the ground.

The story of young Johnny Holmes was one of the strangest to come out of the war. He was only 20, came from an Australian farming family, and had volunteered for flying service on the first day of the war. He was tall, blond, likeable, and irresponsible.

He flew in a squadron of Sopwith biplanes, often carrying an observer who sketched German gun emplacements as Holmes dived low over the trenches. It was invariably Holmes who swooped lower than anyone else.

On the evening of September 16, tracers lit the sky as usual. In a hut by the side of the landing strip, Johnny Holmes and three other Australian pilots were playing poker.

The stakes were high. Since they were all heavily in debt, the game was played largely on credit. At midnight when a senior officer came along and ordered them to douse the lights, Holmes was the heaviest loser.

Unusually serious

In these games no one really expected to get his winnings, but there was a regular charade of writing out I.O.U.s and handing them over.

On this occasion, Holmes wrote his out with care and, handing them over with unusual seriousness, said: "I can't

143

possibly pay you tonight but I will in the morning." His fellow pilots might have wondered where Holmes would find financial backing in the middle of the Marne battlefield, but no one said anything. They took the slips and went to bed.

Friday, September 17, was bright and calm. Holmes and his observer, Richard Jackson, were scheduled to take off first. The rest of the squadron, still warming up their aircraft, watched him taxi off.

The machine had hardly got to a height of three hundred feet when it spiralled into a dive in a way considered impossible unless it was intentionally done. There was a rumble and a sheet of flames as the plane rammed itself into a nearby rocky outcrop.

Struggled with controls

When rescuers reached the spot, both Holmes and Jackson were dead.

But the war went on. Ground staff beckoned Flying Officer Ronald Davidson, another Australian, and a member of the previous night's poker school, to take off. He was flying a double machine with a seat for the observer and dual controls, but the observer's seat was empty.

Davidson rolled the machine forward and took off. He glanced at his gauges and controls: everything seemed normal. Soon the aircraft was droning 500 feet above the trees.

Suddenly men below saw the machine dip and roll. Davidson appeared to be struggling with the controls. Then the engine spluttered and stalled.

Like a stone

The lack of height gave the pilot no chance: the machine fell like a stone. Davidson was dragged from the blazing fuselage and rushed, critically burned, to a field hospital.

An hour later he recovered consciousness. In a whisper, he told an amazing story. As soon as the plane had gained a little height, he felt it dip, as though extra weight had been suddenly added.

He turned and there, sitting in the observer's seat was Johnny Holmes. "As I watched, he switched on the dual control unit and took hold of the joystick. I could feel him pushing against me, forcing the nose down. I could not summon up enough strength . . . there was nothing I could do."

On the face of it, it seemed an unbelievable tale but there was no chance to question Davidson further. He slipped into a coma, and an hour later he died.

Request refused

Back at the airstrip, a further drama was unfolding. The third member of the poker school, Flying Officer Owen Norris, not knowing the fate of Davidson but realizing something strange was going on, had asked to be excused from taking a machine up that morning. The request was refused.

At 11:55 A.M., Norris took another two-seater plane out of its makeshift hanger and taxied it across the rough airstrip. Again the observer's seat was empty. Again, when the plane was about 500 feet from the ground, it began to roll and sway; again the engine surged and died as Norris obviously tried to gain height and was in some way being prevented.

Again the engine spluttered and died. The plane plunged back on to the grass.

Norris was alive when picked up. He lived just long enough to tell those around him that Johnny Holmes had been sitting behind him and had wrenched the controls away. . . .

SHE DREAMED OF THE DEATH OF HER SON

And he hadn't even been born!

The dream of Mrs. Porteus is the most celebrated of all recorded prophetic visions. Childless at the time, she dreamed of her son—his childhood, manhood and, finally, his death at the hands of a mob in Edinburgh. And every detail was to come uncannily and tragically true.

THE DREAM of Mrs. Mary Porteus shook her awake and she lay in the darkness wide-eyed and shivering with fright.

She woke her husband and told him what she had seen. He did his best to comfort her and to persuade her that there was nothing to fear. He did not succeed. Mary Porteus lay awake for the rest of the night, endlessly reconstructing her nightmare.

It had been vivid and horrific. It was also to become the most celebrated prophetic vision in the history of the occult.

For the dream Mrs. Porteus had one night in 1705 foretold in uncannily accurate detail the life and death of a son then unborn. The story may be 250 years old but it still takes its place among the classic tales of the inexplicable.

In her dream Mrs. Porteus saw before her a small boy who she felt instinctively was to be her first-born child. He was in a nursery playing with toys and she was fondly watching him.

Jeering crowd

The child turned into a young man, a soldier in the army. He was about to embark for service abroad and Mrs. Porteus saw herself and her husband weeping as he boarded the ship.

Again the scene changed and the young soldier was back in Edinburgh in the uniform of a captain of the city guard. He was supervising an execution. As the criminal was hanged, the crowd jeered and pelted the executioner with stones.

The guard captain ordered his men to fire on the mob and dozens of men fell dead.

The scene changed again and she saw her son, locked in a prison cell. In a final sequence, an infuriated mob armed with muskets and swords broke into the prison, seized Captain Porteus, dragged him into the street . . . and hanged him.

Then the vision ended. Mrs. Porteus woke up sobbing hysterically.

Joined the Army

In due course, she gave birth to a son who proved to be exactly like the child in the vision. The greatest care was taken in his upbringing and when old enough he was sent to the best school in Edinburgh.

John Porteus was a headstrong child, fearless and with little affection for his parents. They wanted him to be a doctor, but he scorned the profession and against his family's wishes enlisted in the army.

The scene of his departure was an exact replica of the episode in the dream. In fact, the vision she had had nearly 20 years earlier flashed across Mary Porteus's mind as she and her husband both in tears watched the hard-faced young man board the ship for service in the West Indies.

He was abroad for five years and on his return, left the army and lived for some years in London. All this time, he never wrote to his parents, who had left their old home and were living in a village ten miles outside Edinburgh.

Three day hunt

Porteus returned to the city in 1735 and through friends' influence was appointed to the command of the City Guard, with the rank of Captain. His grim disposition and complete lack of humanity made him universally feared and disliked.

He had long since discarded his parents, and when his father died in 1736 he never bothered to attend the funeral or to even send a wreath or message of condolence.

A few weeks afterwards, Porteus and his men were called out one night to search for two smugglers who had broken into a Customs building and stolen goods which had previously been seized from them by Revenue officers.

This was a capital offence and Porteus hounded them relentlessly. Three days later the men, Robert Walker and Andrew Stuart, were found on the coast, brutally manhandled, and brought back to Edinburgh.

The case was by no means cut and dried: there was a good deal of doubt cast on whether the men had committed any offence. They claimed they had paid duty on the goods and were entitled to claim them.

Dread day

After a brisk trial before Lord Justice Thomson, they were convicted and sentenced to be hanged on the following Monday.

On the Sunday before the dread day, Walker and Stuart were on their way to church to hear prayers for their souls, when Stuart succeeded in escaping. He ran up a side-street and the large crowd, clearly in favor of the escape, obstructed Porteus and his men until Stuart was out of sight.

The scene of Walker's execution was exactly as Mrs. Porteus had seen it in her vision.

The smuggler, with his arms bound, stood on the scaffold. Next to him was the executioner, and nearby the grim unmoved figure of Captain Porteus.

Eager for trouble

A large and restless crowd had gathered for the hanging. It made no secret of the fact that its sympathies lay with the prisoner and there were catcalls and angry cries.

Around the gallows, the City Guard stood with loaded muskets ready for any trouble. Porteus, always eager for violence, had drawn his pistol and was thoughtfully fingering the trigger.

As Walker was hanged, the executioner was pelted with grass and stones. This was all Porteus had been waiting for: he ordered his men to fire on the crowd.

A dozen people fell amid a shower of ball-shot. Porteus himself fired at a young man on the fringe of the crowd, killing him instantly.

The brawl was broken up by the arrival of a battalion of soldiers. The next day Porteus himself was arrested, brought before the Lords of Judiciary, found guilty of murder and sentenced to death.

Celebration toast

A week before the execution he was reprieved, and Edinburgh seethed with anger. The night before his release some friends arrived at the prison to celebrate the reprieve.

They were drinking a celebration toast when the noise of

sledge-hammers and axes was heard: a mob was breaking into the jail.

The doors were forced open and before Porteus had time to escape, he was seized by rioters, dragged along Edinburgh High Street and before a huge and near hysterical mob, hanged in the Market.

And so it was that the vision of Mrs. Mary Porteus had, in every detail, come uncannily and tragically true.

TWO CAPTAINS ABOARD—AND ONE WAS A GHOST!

Was this a legend of the sea come true?

The men of the British freighter Carlton *buried their captain. The next day he returned to haunt them. And eventually a man sacrificed his career rather than share the bridge with a ghost.*

THE BLUEY-GREEN water of the Arabian Sea rolled sluggishly and lethargically stirred the British freighter *Carlton* as she lay, engines silent, under the vicious sun.

Pitch bubbled between the deck planking. Under an awning on the after-deck, most of the crew had gathered. Despite the heat, they were wearing their best uniforms. They listened respectfully as the first mate read briefly from the Bible.

Then four men lifted an improvised chute and hung it over the rail. There was a long sighing swish, a flash of white wood, and a pale green plume of water. The men of the *Carlton* had buried their Captain.

In the deckhouse, the duty officer reached for the telegraph, the boatswain spun the wheel. Life returned to the ship. But the men on the deck were still looking out over the side.

They were watching the first stirrings of a phenomenon which was to turn the *Carlton* into a ship of doom, its crew into a bunch of frightened men.

Scream of pain

It was to become a ship with two captains, yet only one was of this world.

It was on the night of May 4, 1958 when tragedy struck the *Carlton*.

She had come at a leisurely 10 knots all day down the Red Sea, and as night fell and the binnacle light went on in the deckhouse, the Master, Captain Norman Harrison, left the bridge and climbed down to the engine room for a routine chat with the chief engineer.

The paradoxical calm of that roaring hell-hole was shattered at three minutes before midnight by the screech of high-pressure steam and a human scream of pain. A pipe had fractured and let loose a cannonade of scalding steam which threw Captain Harrison across the engine room. By the time they picked him up, he was dead.

Seagull hovered

They buried him two days' sail from Aden, and the First Mate, Andrew Cooper read the burial service. He had served with Captain Harrison for ten years. He was strangely perturbed, like the rest of the crew, by what happened when the Captain's coffin slid into the sea.

A seagull detached itself from a wheeling flock and hovered over the place where the coffin had sunk. It hovered for fully half a minute, then it turned flew away slowly and alone. There was a murmur among the older men. In seaman's lore, there are several superstitions about the souls of dead sailors being transferred into seagulls.

Everyone was glad when the engines throbbed again and the ship continued her journey.

First hint

Andrew Cooper had cabled the owners about the incident. There would be an inquiry when the ship reached Aden. In the meantime, he would act as Captain.

At dawn the following morning came the first hint that Cooper was not the only captain aboard the *Carlton*.

A group of seamen repairing a lifeboat fitting near the stern happened to glance at the bridge. They saw the figure of a man looking out over the starboard horizon. They saw the glint of braid on his arm. They knew also that Captain Cooper was not on watch.

The figure turned and the men stared, aghast, at the face of Captain Norman Harrison. Cooper was brought from his cabin. He too saw the figure clearly. As he started towards the bridge steps, the figure went into the deckhouse.

Figure had gone

But when Cooper burst in, there was no one there but the boatswain and the officer of the watch, and they had seen nothing out of the ordinary.

Later that day, the figure was seen again, standing on the foc's'le looking out to sea. The sailor who saw it, rushed to tell Cooper, but by the time he looked again, the figure had gone.

By now the crew was nervy and on edge. A deputation approached Cooper requesting that speed be increased and that a priest be asked to exorcise the ship when it reached Aden.

Cooper refused. He did not believe in ghosts. Captain Harrison was dead and lying in his coffin 100 miles away at the bottom of the Arabian Sea.

On May 7, the *Carlton* docked in Aden Harbor. It was dawn before she was secured and Captain Cooper went below to his berth.

At 7 A.M. he was awakened by a vigorous shake of the shoulder. This was routine; Captain Harrison always did it when they were changing watches.

The ritual of years was fixed in Cooper's subconscious. Automatically he clambered from his bunk and reached for his shirt. Then, instantaneously, he was awake and rigid with disbelief.

The arm which shook him, and the voice, belonged to Captain Harrison. He turned and saw the door closing slowly. He ran and looked out into the companionway. Inevitably, no one was there.

If the experience was an illusion it was an expensive one for Andrew Cooper. He cabled his London owners and declined the master's appointment. He had waited ten years for his first command and now he threw it away.

But he was happy to let someone else share the captaincy of the *Carlton* with the ghost of Norman Harrison.

LONELY GHOST BRINGS ORDEAL BY FLOOD

200 times it has wrecked this family's home . . .

Every time the Whittock-Knott family leave their home, a mystery wrecker moves in. Nearly 200 times in a year it has been damaged by fire and flood. Yet no one can find anything wrong with the house or its fittings.

Mrs. Heidi Whittock-Knott alighted from the village bus and walked up the lane to her neat stone-built house. It had been newly decorated and the paintwork glistened and shone.

She placed her shopping bag on the step and unlocked the front door. Then she screamed. Water was pouring down the ceiling and the walls. It flooded down the stairs, over the floor and swirled round her feet.

She rushed into the house to see what had happened. But no taps had been left on, no pipe appeared to have burst, the water-tank had not overflowed.

That was over a year ago. Since then, the house in the West of England village of Farmborough has been flooded mysteriously 140 times.

Secret fires have burned furniture and fittings on over 50 occasions. Yet police and technicians can't find anything wrong with the house.

"Nothing wrong"

Psychical experts have spent weeks examining Mrs. Whittock-Knott's home. They believe that the havoc is caused by a lonely ghost, a poltergeist who resents being left alone and causes the damage out of pique. There is no other explanation which stands any possible examination, and the damage only occurs when the house in unoccupied.

The phantom floods of Number Six, Hunt Street Road, were first regarded as accidents. A new plumbing system had recently been installed and it was thought that it might have developed teething troubles.

A team of plumbers descended on the house and systematically checked every fitting, pipe and joint. Then they told Mrs. Whittock-Knott: "We can find absolutely nothing wrong."

The next day it happened again. Neighbors rushed in and

helped mop up the swirling flood. They helped Mrs. Whittock-Knott search for a plumbing leak. Again the water seemed to have come from nowhere.

Fateful day

For the next few weeks, plumbers and engineers virtually lived in the house. The water tank was replaced and all pipes minutely checked. But as soon as the house was empty, the deluge began again.

And recently a new terror has come to the house in the quiet lane: a creeping smokeless fire which burns curtains, chairs, furniture and scorches wallpaper.

The violence of the lonely ghost started two years after the Whittock-Knotts had moved into the house.

It was seemingly sparked off when builders and plumbers came to make structural alterations and install the new water system. They disturbed the 40-year-old stone and mortar—and something more ominous too. The day after the workmen left the ordeal by fire and water began.

On that fateful afternoon, 32-year-old Mrs. Whittock-Knott locked the front door and went shopping. Her lorry-driver husband Ernest was at work, her four children were at school.

Odd feeling

She recalls: "I couldn't believe my eyes when I came home. Everything was soaked. Carpets and wallpaper were ruined. Two days later, the same thing happened again. But we couldn't find anything wrong with the plumbing."

After months of misery, she sought the aid of a psychical researcher. He investigated the house's history and uncovered some uncanny facts: when it was being constructed a builder had dropped dead on the site, another had gone mad, and another went bankrupt.

The expert found there was a strange atmosphere in the house. He reported: "There would be a sudden clamminess and an odd feeling of unrest in the air." He kept watch on the house when it was left empty.

He heard nothing out of the ordinary, yet when Mrs. Whittock-Knott returned, water was again pouring from the hall into the living room and kitchen. And again there was no feasible explanation.

Not an accident

After this, the mystery took an ominous turn. Whatever it was that tyrannized the household, was becoming vicious. One day workmen came to the house to check the water system for the 28th time and fit the fifth new tank.

The tank was lying securely on the landing. It took two men to lift it into position. Yet coming back into the house after a tea-break, one of the plumbers said, "That water tank has moved."

That afternoon it moved again. While the men's backs were turned it moved over four feet along the landing and heaved itself over the edge of the stairs. Mrs. Whittock-Knott, walking across the hall below, screamed and fled as the heavy tank tumbled towards her missing her by inches.

Yet she also testified that it could not have been an accident—the men were working yards away.

Strange ordeal

Not content with water and violence, the phantom has now added flames to its armory of fear.

One afternoon Mrs. Whittock-Knott came home to find that instead of floods, her kitchen curtains had burned right up to the wire. The wallpaper on either side of the window was scorched—but there was no sign or smell of smoke. Furniture had been scorched, obviously by terrific heat—but there was no obvious source of fire.

Now the Whittock-Knotts wait fearfully for the next manifestations of the violent ghost. They cannot sell the house—who would buy such a load of trouble?

They remain there, a baffled family undergoing a strange modern ordeal by fire and flood.

FOURTEEN MILE RIDE OF THE INVISIBLE MAN

And he had been dead for three days!

For fourteen miles, a bearded man dressed in deep black rode with Colonel Roger Marsh. Yet no one but the Colonel could see him. Seconds after they parted, Marsh saw him again—as a three-day-old corpse. . . .

OLD Charles Norman, lodgekeeper on the High Ashley Estate in the midst of England's rolling Sussex Downs, climbed out of his arm-chair and peered through his kitchen window as he heard a horse approaching the high iron gates.

Along the drive came the dog-cart of his master, Colonel Roger Marsh, the bay gelding stepping lightly along the gravel, and slowing to a walk as the cart approached the gates.

Old Charles groped hurriedly for his boots and hat: he mustn't keep the colonel waiting. But even as he opened the kitchen door he heard the gates clash closed and the wheels of the dog-cart rattle away along the drive.

How could the colonel possibly have opened the gate,

driven through and closed it behind him with such speed? Norman looked again through his window at the departing cart.

Yes, the colonel was alone . . . yet he seemed to be talking to someone! In fact, Colonel Roger Marsh *had* a passenger—a man who sat with him in the dog-cart for over 14 miles but who could be seen by no one but himself. . . .

No illusion

This macabre drive took place on September 14, 1903, when Colonel Marsh was driving from his estate to spend the day with a neighbor. But the passenger was no illusion. His added weight made the horse strain on hills; his suitcase stood stolidly on the floor of the cart.

And he got down to open and close three sets of gates during the three-hour journey.

It was about 9 A.M. when Colonel Marsh packed an overnight bag and left his Jacobean country house to visit his friend Sir Frank Lewis who lived across the valley. The air was brisk as he bowled along the beech-lined drive and a few leaves were already wafting from the boughs. He had to pass through several miles of parkland before he came to the first lodge.

At one point the road left the trees and curved over a small bridge spanning a stream. There was a footpath nearby leading to the village of Edgingly. It was on this bridge that Colonel Marsh first saw the man.

A stranger

He was sallow-skinned, heavily bearded and dressed in unrelieved black. He had a small leather case by his side and was leaning over the parapet of the bridge gazing into the water.

Hearing the sound of the cart he turned and watched it approach. The colonel recalled what happened then: "I noticed he looked tired and drawn. I stopped the cart and offered to give him a lift. He thanked me, put his bag on the floor and climbed in. I distinctly felt the cart sway as he climbed up."

The colonel introduced himself and the passenger said that he was Matthew Thomas, a stranger to the district, staying at the inn in Edgingly before moving on to Brighton.

They drove for some time until they came to the lodge occupied by Charles Norman. As there seemed no one near the gate, Thomas climbed down, pushed it open, closed it after the cart had passed through, and got up again besides Colonel Marsh.

Hurried inside

On several occasions the colonel passed people he knew. Once he stopped to pass the time of day with a clergyman, the Rev. John Stoppard. Later, Stoppard stated emphatically that the dog-cart contained no one but Colonel Marsh.

Just before lunch, they reached the village of Edgingly and approached the Spread Eagle Inn, where Thomas said he was staying. There was an unusual number of people outside the inn, and Marsh saw two constables and a police inspector in discussion with a man he knew to be the district coroner.

The colonel pulled the cart off the road and stopped near the inn door. A servant came out and grasped the horse's head while the two men climbed down. Without a word, Thomas grasped his bag and hurried into the building.

Thoroughly confused

"Is that man staying here?" the colonel asked the stable lad.

"What man, sir?"

"The man I drove up with."

"I haven't seen anyone," the lad replied. "You drove up alone, sir."

Thoroughly confused, Colonel Marsh sent for the landlord. He gave a description of his passenger and asked if there was anyone of that description in the house.

The landlord looked grave. "Indeed there is, sir," he said. He led the way upstairs and unbolted the door of a room.

Lying on the bed was the man to whom Colonel Marsh had given a lift. He had been dead, said the landlord, for three days. In fact, the people crowding the inn courtyard had been attending an inquest on his death.

The body had been found drowned close to the bridge where Colonel Marsh had stopped to give the man a lift. His death was a mystery; the water was shallow and the bank not steep.

There the matter rested. A centuries-old folk lore myth, that the soul always returns to the body once in every 24 hours before a funeral is the only possible clue to this mysterious and macabre story.

THE PLANE WITH MURDER IN ITS HEART . . .

Twice it had killed—now it struck again . . .

A man had died at the controls of the silver airliner; a mechanic had been killed working on it. Now, incredibly, the plane seemed to have a will of its own. It defied its pilot—as if unseen hands were guiding it to disaster.

"EMERGENCY . . . Emergency . . ." the words over loud-speakers shook the silence of the airport control tower at Gander, Newfoundland.

Already the alarm bells were shrilling; fire tenders and ambulances tore out on to the runway.

The cause of the emergency was there for all to see. A Lockheed Constellation airliner, brimming with fuel for a trans-Atlantic crossing, hovered lamely over the runway, its number one port engine ablaze.

The tenders streamed along, trying to catch up. Then in terrible slow-motion the plane bounced back on to the runway, slewed and slithered among the foam sprayed by firemen and jarred to a halt.

For a moment Captain Bob Norman, a 38-year-old Canadian, leaned heavily on his forearms, his head bowed over the control yoke. Then he was up, leading his scared passengers to safety, watching fire-fighters smother the flames in foam.

He took the incident calmly. It merely confirmed his opinion that the big silver airliner AHEM-4 was determined to kill him.

What was wrong?

The date was July 9, 1947. A year ago to the day, Captain Arthur Lewis had collapsed and died at the controls of AHEM-4 as it droned high above the Atlantic. Twelve months before that, a fitter at Prestwick Airport had stepped into Ahem-4's lethal propellors and was hacked instantly to death.

It seemed the plane wanted to keep the anniversary.

Flight Controller J. S. Gaskill said as much when he hurried down to meet Norman. Already mechanics were swarming over the plane. Everything in the aircraft had been checked and doublechecked before take-off. What had gone wrong?

In six hours the plane had been minutely examined, refueled, and the engine replaced, and a new crew detailed.

Gaskill returned to his office to find Norman there. "If anyone takes that plane up," said the pilot, "it must be me." Eventually Gaskill agreed. Just before midnight Norman and his crew walked back over the tarmac to AHEM-4.

Moment of truth

The passengers, determinedly relaxed and chatting gaily, settled in their seats as the plane's engines spluttered into life and the plane taxied out towards the runway lights.

At the edge of the runway, Norman stopped and tested each engine with minute care, studying the dials for the slightest sign of malfunction. Everything seemed perfect. Nevertheless they worked through the complete printed check list. Norman was not taking the slightest chance.

Then each member of the crew answered in turn, "Ready, Captain."

To the layman they would have seemed almost bored; to a professional, the tension could have been cut with a knife. They all knew the moment of truth was now very near. Norman swivelled his seat forward. Co-pilot Louis Ford made a last minute survey of the dials. Then Norman said, "Give me take-off power."

The plane shuddered and strained, held firmly on the brakes until the roaring engines built up full power, the exhaust-pipes glowing hot in the dusk. Then the captain lifted his feet.

The runway lights began to roll past, slowly at first, then in rapid flicks. Norman bent forward, left hand on the nose-wheel steering column, right resting lightly on the throttles. He was listening intently to the engines.

Dreaded message

Ford sang out the increasing speed: "Ninety . . . one hundred . . . one five . . ." Quickly the captain shifted his hands on to the main controls ready for flight.

At 145 m.p.h. Norman hauled back on the control yoke and the heavy plane came away from the ground. Ford, still listening intently to the port engines, heard the captain's orders: "Up gear, up flaps," and obeyed them automatically. The landing gear locked into place, the overheated engines relaxed a shade.

Then on the instrument panel a red light flared. A bell clanged so loudly that it drowned the engines. From the engineer came the message that filled them all with dread. The chance in a million had been realized. "Captain," he shouted, "port number one is on fire."

They couldn't believe it. But it was true. The engine which had been installed only hours before was a mass of fire. Norman pressed a switch and fire extinguishers under the wings poured chemicals into the burning engine. Almost instantly, the red light went out and the bell stopped. The fire seemed to be out.

But a hideous obstacle now confronted them. Straight ahead lay a block of flats. Although only five storeys high, the roofs were above the aircraft's nose.

Last chance

Now with one engine dead, Norman dare not bank steeply. There was only one salvation: to climb.

The captain eased back on the controls and a faint shudder ran along the plane. To Norman it signalled certain death from an impending stall. He now knew that without doubt AHEM-4 was out to kill him. The plane would not climb.

Only one weapon remained—a resumption of take-off power on the remaining three engines.

Take-off power imposed terrible heat and strain, and could be used for a maximum of two minutes. That's all they would have to master the plane with death in its heart.

With the increased power, Norman once again eased the controls. They did not respond. The gauges showed that everything was normal. But the control yoke was moving down instead of up: it was as though some unearthly hands were on it, guiding the plane to disaster.

End of the story

In vain, Norman struggled. Then Louis Ford, crouching at his side, did a courageous and dangerous thing. He reached forward and grasped the control yoke. With their combined strength, it began to move back. Slowly the opposing force weakened, the aircraft's nose rose a fraction, and AHEM-4 swept over the roofs with feet to spare.

Half an hour later, after jettisoning fuel, the airliner touched down uneventfully at the airport. Whatever it was that was out for Norman's blood did not try again that night.

But that was not the end of the story. On July 10, 1949, headlines blazed with reports of an aircrash outside Chicago. The undercarriage collapsed while the plane was coming in to land. Nine passengers and the crew of four lost their lives.

The plane was AHEM-4 . . . the Captain's name was Bob Norman.

HE SET A TRAP FOR A MONSTER

And became its first victim . . .

*For over 40 years, the story of the Loch Watten monster
has intrigued investigators. It obsessed, and then killed,
the man who hunted it. Colonel Trimble was determined
that the monster should die—but in circumstances that
were both macabre and mysterious, it was he who became the victim of the trap he set.*

IT WAS a bright spring day, and steely sunshine glinted over
the mountains of Caithness when Colonel Arthur Trimble first
saw the monster of Loch Watten.

The monster's eyes were slits in a huge squat head, and
its body, which loomed under the rippling water, appeared
at least 20 feet wide. . . . It observed him for several seconds.
He even had time to take a photograph of it.

The phenomenon of the monster of Loch Watten pre-
occupied Colonel Trimble throughout the spring of 1923.
The obsession turned to hatred, then to fear It turned to
stark terror on the night that the monster killed him. . . .

The story of the Colonel and the monster has intrigued
writers and investigators for 40 years. Slowly, the story has
been pieced together and an incredible tale it makes. But
there are cold facts in abundance which no one can dispute.

The saga began on April 21 when the Colonel, who had
retired from the Army the previous year, was walking with his
spaniel Bruce across the small estate he had bought in the
Scottish highlands—and which was bordered by Loch Watten.

Rushed forward

He had heard of the monster—"The Serpent" the locals called it—but he had never seen it and didn't expect to. Now there it was before him. As he watched in shocked surprise, the Colonel's hands instinctively groped for the camera around his neck. Swiftly adjusting shutter and lens to the April light, he focused on the target of a lifetime.

Then as his finger closed on the shutter release, the dog, which up to now had stood silently at his side, rushed forward into the water. There was a splash and a huge flurry. Trimble pressed his shutter firmly on the melee in his viewfinder and hoped he had not been too late. He made out the dog splashing through a bed of reeds to the shore; of the monster there was no sign.

Staked his claim

Colonel Trimble returned to his house and wrote a report of what he had seen; then he took the film from his camera and sent it to the local chemist's. Perhaps if the print showed the monster in fair detail, he would send it to *The Times* with a cautious letter on the subject.

Later, he might write to the Royal Society, the Freshwater Biological Association, and other bodies to stake his claim for discovering some new forgotten species. For Trimble did not believe in the supernatural.

The next day, he got the film back. There on the enlarged print he had asked for, slightly blurred yet completely visible, was the head and neck of the monster.

Eagerly Colonel Trimble wrote his letter to *The Times,* enclosing the photograph, and went down to the village to post it. By the end of the week, he expected, Loch Watten would be as celebrated as Loch Ness.

Deeply upset

Now most of his day was spent in vigil near the Loch waiting with his camera for the monster's next appearance. Apart from a few mysterious ripples he saw nothing, but it did nothing to decrease the Colonel's enthusiasm which was fast bordering an obsession.

On the evening of May 1, his housekeeper Mrs. Doris Dougal reported that Bruce, the spaniel, was missing. They were searching the house and grounds without success when the Colonel's nearest neighbor, Dr. Robert McArdish, arrived with news of the dog. He said he had been fishing at the loch and caught sight of Bruce swimming a long way from the shore. Suddenly there had been a flurry and the dog had vanished.

"That thing must die," Trimble told the doctor. "The loch is technically mine, so I must do it." The doctor wondered what he meant. He assumed the loss of his dog had deeply upset the Colonel.

The next day Trimble made his plans for the killing of the Serpent. He sent Mrs. Dougal to the village to order a large piece of fresh horsemeat.

Set a trap

In the evening, after spending most of the day in his garage, Colonel Trimble emerged at evening carrying a bulky sack. He strode over the sloping moorlands towards the loch.

As the moon was rising a dinghy tossed on the surface of the water. Crouching over the gunwale, Trimble completed his mission. Over the side with fifty fathoms of rope and a marker buoy went the horsemeat—and inside lay a huge steel hook. Colonel Trimble had set a monster trap.

The next day he went back to the shores of Loch Watten and the buoy still bobbed where he had placed it.

On the evening of May 4, the Colonel told Mrs. Dougal

he was taking a walk down to the loch.

Heard a sound

She thought it strange because it was almost dark—but then, he had been behaving rather strangely.

At 9:30 P.M. he had not returned and she went to the door of the house. Through the darkness she heard a distant scream. She ran for the gardener who lived at an adjoining cottage and together they set out for the loch.

They found Arthur Trimble lying among the reeds in shallow water. He was dead. A sharpened spike, attached to a long length of rope had apparently pierced his heart.

And through the gloom, Mrs. Dougal could hear the sound of something—something large—swimming away from the shore.

HIS CHRISTMAS DREAM CAME TRUE

And it had a nightmare ending . . .

> *The nightmare of Rene Barbot was always the same: a mutilated figure lay under hospital lights. But on the day when it all came true, the real-life ending was more horrific than anything he had ever dreamed.*

RENE BARBOT WAS an accountant in a Marseilles bank. At 32, he had a steadiness and a sobriety one expects to find in a far older man. He had also a complete lack of imagination.

His wife Marie, five years his junior, was a very different personality, nervous, sensitive, and animated; she sometimes had a fleeting yearning for a life a little more gay, a little more eventful. But it passed. Rene was a good husband; she had a lot to be thankful for.

168

They had their three-year-old son Cyrille; then there was her uncle Jules who rented a first floor room and provided them with a little money for luxuries. Things could indeed be worse.

Then in the early days of December 1954, into the uncomplicated routine life of the Barbot family came something strange and inexplicable. Rene Barbot, the placid head of the house, began to have nightmares.

Or to be more precise, a nightmare—for his dream was always the same.

Always the same

He would wake shaking and incoherent and lie restlessly awake for hours in the darkness reconstructing the horrific scenes which as the nights passed came as familiar to him as his own bedroom.

The venue was always the same: he was in a white room with an overhead light. On a table in the center lay a figure covered in a sheet, on its back with its knees crooked up. The face was exposed, but mutilated and unrecognizable.

Then followed a spine-chilling charade in which a diabolical figure seized the body and carried it off through flickering sheets of flame.

On the first two or three occasions, Marie could not get out of her husband what had happened. Eventually he told her. His whole body shook as the words poured from him.

He dreaded to go to sleep. He would spend the nights reading or listening to the radio. But inevitably sleep crept upon him, and when it did, the dream was always there.

Flood of weeping

The recurring nightmare began to have a visible physical effect upon Rene Barbot. He lost several pounds in weight and his healthy complexion became gray and drawn. His disposition changed: he snapped at his family and refused to see his relations and friends.

Christmas was approaching, and Marie Barbot went about her preparations with a heavy heart. Her husband, now on sick leave from his bank, sat brooding at home, oblivious of everything but his dream and its possible meaning.

On December 15, Jules Marchal, coming home from his job in a solicitor's office, found his niece in tears. He had long been aware of the change in the household, but nothing had been said about it, and he didn't care to ask.

Now in a flood of weeping, Marie told her uncle the whole story. Together they decided there was but one course of action. Rene must see a psychiatrist.

Classic symptoms

Rene had no intentions of seeing a psychiatrist but after a particularly horrific nightmare on December 16, he was persuaded to change his mind.

The next day, Jules Marchal booked an appointment for Rene with Dr. Marc de Sainte, a leading French psychiatrist and an enthusiastic researcher into the phenomena of extrasensory perception. De Sainte recognized in Barbot's story all the ingredients of precognition: an identifiable impression of a coming disaster. Yet he had no intention of telling his patient so.

Instead, he explained that the nightmares had all the classic symptoms of an impending nervous breakdown. There was absolutely nothing to worry about. If the obsession with the dreams could be mastered, the dreams themselves would go.

Slightly reassured, Barbot went home. From that day, his condition improved. He became more cheerful and returned to work. On December 20, he and Jules Marchal decorated the house for Christmas. The nightmare had not recurred.

Call from the police

"I really feel more like my old self," he told his wife. "I can't think why I got so upset about a mere dream."

But the nightmare had not ended. In fact, it had hardly begun.

On the afternoon of Christmas Eve after the bank had closed, the accountants and clerks were invited into the manager's room for the customary Christmas drink.

Through the hum of conversation and laughter a telephone rang. The call was for Rene Barbot; it was from the police. A man, laden with Christmas parcels had stepped from a tramcar in the Boulevard Lazaret into the path of a fast-moving car.

White room

Rene's name and address had been found in his wallet. Hurriedly, Barbot excused himself, left the bank and caught a cab to the Central Hospital. He was met by a nurse and taken to a pre-operating room to identify the casualty. He entered a door—and there before him was the scene of his terrible dream.

There was the white room with the overhead light. On a table in the center was the sight he had seen a dozen times: a figure lying on its back, covered in a sheet, its knees crooked, and its face exposed but mutilated and unrecognizable.

All that was missing was the symbolic figure struggling to carry the body away. But that came too. Jules Marchal died before Barbot left the hospital.

KILLED BY THE MAN HE HAD MURDERED!

Just 20 years later to the day!

Deep in the heart of Australia's Great Dividing Range, a human hand appeared through a waterfall. It was the start of one of the most macabre classics of the unknown ever recorded. For the hand belonged to a man who had been dead for four years—slain at a meeting with two men he had murdered 20 years before.

EVERYBODY loved George Woodfall. As a benefactor, and genial friend of anyone in trouble, he had no equal in Sydney, Australia. When he disappeared on March 3, 1901, it caused a sensation.

He was never seen alive again. After two years a monument was raised to his memory and his name and his deeds became part of the past. But that was by no means the end of George Woodfall.

Amid a glow of eerie light, two witnesses were to see his body cavorting in a horrific dance of death.

They were to find his uncovered grave guarded by two skeletons. And they were to find a confession which told of a meeting with two dead men: a meeting from which he never returned.

The story was fantastic: yet it was told by men of undoubted integrity—a famous scientist and a distinguished priest.

Their reports of what happened on that October day in 1905 stand today as inexplicable classics of the unknown, still studied by students of psychic phenomena.

Thunder rolled

The police made a thorough investigation of Woodfall's disappearance but no clues were found. His affairs were in order, his home life appeared to have been happy; his business was prosperous.

Four years went by. Then, in October 1905, the Rev. Charles Power, priest of the church of St. Chrysostom, Redfern, Sydney, and his friend William Rowley, who envisaged and designed the whole canal system of New South Wales, went for a camping holiday on the mountains of the Great Dividing Range.

On October 20, in the very heart of the mountains, they were searching for a spot to camp for the night. They descended into a long gully and soon came upon a pretty glade fringing a deep pool into which a waterfall thundered from high rocks. It was the ideal spot.

Night was falling as they lit a fire and cooked supper.

Soon the sky became overcast as thunderclouds began to roll. Suddenly Power gripped his companion's arm. He was shaking uncontrollably.

Hid his face

"Look . . ." he said. Rowley turned. Out of the gloom, high up among the lashing foam of the waterfall, had appeared a human hand.

It was the hand of a dead man. As it waved and beckoned a second hand, withered and gruesome like itself, came through the water. Struggling as it were into material shape came two arms.

Power wrote later about what happened next: "As I stood, my mouth agape with horror and every nerve tingling, there, in ghastly completeness, stood a man. But what a man!

"It was a corpse endowed with life . . . The awful thing

173

writhed and rocked with what appeared to be paroxysms of anguish, now standing erect, now falling on to its knees.

"I could bear no more and hid my face in my hands. When I looked again the apparition had vanished."

Spasm of terror

Not surprisingly, the men passed a troubled night. Next day, equipped with lanterns, they decided to explore the caves that lay near the waterfall.

"Of one thing I am firmly convinced," said Power. "Such a terrifying spectacle would never have been allowed to appear before us without some reason."

He led the way into the caves. Soon they found themselves in a long broad passage which wound its way into the side of the mountain. Eventually, it opened into a huge cave.

Power's narrative goes on: "By now we could hear a roaring noise. It was obvious we were in the rocks under the waterfall.

"We passed through a jagged hole into another chamber. I walked first carrying the largest lantern. Suddenly a spasm of terror shook me from head to foot.

Two skeletons

"I fell back against Rowley and clung to him trembling. 'Quick, let us go back,' I shouted. 'This is no place for us!' Holding out the lantern I pointed straight ahead.

"Immediately in front of us yawned an open grave. The earth flung up on each side had grown hard and caked in the years that had rolled by since it was first dug.

"On each side sat a skeleton. Gathering up our courage we stepped forward and peered into the pit. We saw another body. In one glance we recognized the face of the man we had seen in the waterfall the precious night."

The dead hands were around a small metal box. Gently Rowley pried up the fingers and opened the lid. Inside the box was a folded piece of paper.

Together the men read, by the light of their lanters, the confession of George Woodfall. Twenty years earlier, he had murdered two men after a dispute over a gold claim.

Violent souls

He buried them in a cave near the waterfall. The years went by. Then one night in March 1901 he was awakened by a voice. "We shall expect you tomorrow," it said. Woodfall realized that it would be the 20th anniversary of the killings. He felt he must go back to the cave.

The confession ended: "I must make one more visit to that place of bloodstained memories, and when I return I will give myself up. I will place this confession in the hands of the authorities. Then it may be that my tortured soul will find peace at last."

Rowley and Power buried the skeletons together in the grave and heaped earth over them. Power recited the burial service. Then they turned away and left the cave.

The confession was turned over to the police. But to their dying day, the two men refused to disclose the whereabouts of the grave. "The violent souls," said Power, "should be allowed to seek peace at last."

The place has never been found: the fate of George Woodfall is likely to remain a mystery for ever.

FOUR MILES TO LAND—AND HE WALKED IT!

Miracle saved a man who couldn't swim . . .

Rear-gunner Norman Francis grabbed his parachute, made for the escape hatch of the stricken bomber—and leaped to almost certain death. He was a non-swimmer, and the Dutch coast was four miles away. Yet, miraculously, he didn't drown; he found himself walking through the sea to safety.

ONE DAY last June, a middle-aged Englishman hired a rowing boat from a fisherman on the tiny island of Walcheren off the Dutch coast, and sculled, seemingly aimlessly, out to sea.

For three hours he rowed, occasionally stopping to peer into the water, and probe for the sea bed with a pole. Not once did he touch the bottom; the sea all around that coast was dark and deep.

Eventually, Norman Francis returned to the shore, finally convinced of one thing: that more than 20 years earlier, he had been the subject of a miracle. He had *walked*, for nearly four miles, on the surface of the water. . . .

Over the years, he had thought frequently of his miraculous escape when, wounded and unable to swim, he had parachuted into the North Sea, and found something strange and solid beneath his feet.

He had thought that chance must have guided him on to a sandbank, but study of marine charts, and now this on-the-spot check made it quite clear; there were no shoals or sandbanks in the area.

Last dive

So the miracle which saved his life remains as baffling as the night he baled out into the darkness of the sea, convinced he would never watch another day dawn.

Warrant-Officer Norman Francis was 30 on the day he should have died. The Stirling bomber in which he was rear-gunner was droning towards Germany on one of the last raids of the war.

Suddenly, disaster struck, swiftly and with a terrible finality Machine gun bullets from a German fighter raked the plane. And bomber J FOR JOHNNY heeled over for its last dive.

Over the intercom, the pilot ordered: "Bale out. Get cracking, chaps . . . we've had it." Swiftly, Norman Francis grabbed his parachute, closed the transparent doors of his turret, and dived through his escape hatch.

The slipstream caught him, spinning him head over heels, and the wing of the spiraling bomber caught him a vicious blow on the chest as it went by. But before he lapsed into unconsciousness, he jerked at his parachute rip-cord.

His blackout must have lasted only seconds: when he came round, his parachute had opened and he was swaying in the night, ten thousand feet up. Down below, glinting in the moonlight, he could see the dark expanse of the sea.

He tried to control the parachute by pulling on the rigging lines, but it had no effect. Things looked as black as they could be: he was miles from land, he was injured—and he couldn't swim.

The instant he smacked into the sea he pressed the release of his parachute but was instantly tangled in the cords, which took an octopus-like hold on his legs. He kept calm, managed to break free, and shot to the surface.

Later he recalled: "I should have had my Mae West lifejacket on, but like a fool I had taken it off. I always found it too bulky in the turret. I remember thinking: 'I can't swim, so what am I struggling for? . . . I guess this is it.' "

He recalls the icy cold of the water, the smothering darkness, and his thoughts as he struggled for life—a tiny lonely dot in the North Sea. For the first time he panicked.

Told no one

What happened next seemed so fantastic, that for years, Francis told no one about it.

"I reckon I was about four miles out when I fell. I had almost made up my mind to die when . . . I found myself standing on my feet in the water. Or rather, I was standing on one foot. And inside my head it was just as though someone had said, 'Don't worry—you're going to be all right!'

Solid sand

"I was standing on something solid yet soft—I found I was able to walk. Soon I was only up to my knees in water. Although I didn't know it then, every step I took was in the direction of the shore.

"I lost all sense of time. Then the dawn began to break and suddenly I noticed the coastline a long way off—at least two miles . . . on and on—until eventually the substance beneath my feet changed, and became firm sand.

"The next thing I knew I was crawling up the stonework of a breakwater."

He could see a windmill and a couple of whitewashed houses in the distance. It took him another hour to reach them, crawling on his hands and knees. He staggered up the path and banged on a door.

An old Dutchwoman opened it. Francis was given food and medical help—then handed over to the Germans. The Dutch did not want to risk Nazi reprisals by helping an English airman.

A miracle?

Francis spent the rest of the war in a prison camp. For more than 20 years afterwards he nursed the memory of that fantastic night. Eventually, he took time off from his job as a factory foreman and went over to Holland.

He found the very spot he had crawled up the beach. Nothing seemed to have changed. He put on his bathing trunks and waded out. Soon he was out of his depth: there was absolutely nothing to support him.

His investigations in the boat threw no light on the mystery either: as far as he could tell the sea was deep and shoal-free. There seemed no solution to the mystery.

"I had prayed for a miracle," said Francis, "and it came. By what other means could a man possibly walk on the water?"

HAVE THESE CHILDREN BEEN ALIVE BEFORE?

Twins can remember the day they died!

The story of the Pollock twins is perhaps the strongest link in the chain of evidence to support the theory of reincarnation. They talk about events that occurred eight years ago—events that happened to two children who died before the twins were born.

ELEVEN-YEAR-OLD Joanna Pollock and her six-year-old sister Jacqueline skipped gaily down the pavement on their way to Mass. It was a Sunday in May 1957, and the sun was glinting on the pavements of the north-of-England seaside town of Whitley Bay.

Suddenly the peace of the early summer day was shat
tered. A car swept round a corner into the children. Both
were fatally injured.

It was tragically hard for milkman John Pollock and his
wife Florence to accept that their daughters were dead. And
every day it becomes harder.

For the Pollocks are convinced that Joanna and Jacqueline
are back in the little house overlooking the gray North Sea
. . . contained in the bodies of two younger children.

The story of the Pollock twins is already becoming the
strongest link in the chain of evidence to support the theory
of reincarnation. Psychic researchers rate it one of the most
baffling—and intriguing—stories of the decade.

A white scar

Gillian and Jennifer were born seventeen months after
the tragedy. No one has ever discussed with them details of
their sisters' deaths . . . yet they know about the accident
down to the last detail.

And everything they say tallies with the facts. Jennifer,
the younger by ten minutes of the five-year-old twins, is the
image of Jacqueline, the younger of the dead sisters. Photographs show the resemblance clearly.

Since the night she was born, Jennifer has had an unusual
white scar just an inch and a quarter long running along her
forehead. Jacqueline had an identical scar—the result of falling down when she was three years old.

There are other uncanny similarities: Jennifer has a red-
brown birthmark on her hip, about the size of a shilling—
Jacqueline had one exactly the same.

Astounding facts

The Pollocks are constantly noting similarities between

the live children and the two who are dead. For instance, Jennifer likes writing.

Without any prompting she had adopted the peculiar habit of holding her pencil between the middle fingers of her right hand, and propelling it with her fist. Jacqueline did the same thing. . . .

Researchers are intrigued by the evidence Mr. and Mrs. Pollock have to offer. They have interviewed the girls and extracted facts about things and places that Jennifer and Gillian have never experienced or seen but Joanna and Jacqueline had.

Gillian copies Joanna in many ways too. She uses many of the same expressions, has the same walk, the same tendency to lead her sister around by the hand.

But perhaps the most astounding fact is that the girls talk about the accident as if it had happened to them personally.

Gillian speaks frequently of details no one has ever discussed with her.

Evidence piles up

Recently, Mrs. Pollock found Gillian, her hands on Jenniser's shoulders, describing in close detail the injuries Jacqueline suffered in the crash.

Once, after the girls had gone for a walk, a neighbor found them crying by the roadside. They were standing in the precise spot where the tragedy had occurred—and again, no one had told them the exact location.

Jennifer once asked her mother: "What happened to Mr. —? Is he still very upset about the crash?" She mentioned the name of the man who was driving the car, knew where he lived and what sort of vehicle he drove.

"Evidence is continually piling up," says John Pollock, "which confirms my conviction that Jacqueline and Joanna have returned to this earth."

Certainly incidents keep occurring which are impossible

to explain away. "Recently," says the father, "while I was in the loft I came upon a box of toys I had parceled up after the children died.

Strange feeling

"I know for a fact that the twins had never seen the box, and could have no idea of what it contained.

"I decided to give them the toys. Immediately I opened the box, Gillian pounced on a little toy wringer for squeezing out washed dolls' clothes and excitedly cried out, 'Look, Daddy—here's my wringer again.'

"The toy had belonged to Joanna and it was her favorite plaything." It is incidents like these—and there are plenty of them—which are bringing experts reluctantly to the conclusion that the Pollock twins have walked the earth before.

One of the last to be convinced was their father. He is a Roman Catholic, and that faith does not accept the theory of reincarnation. But after the children died he had a strange feeling that they would be replaced in the family by twin girls.

Mrs. Pollock scoffed at the idea—so did the doctors who examined her. They could detect only one heartbeat. But twins were born.

Baffling story

At first Mrs. Pollock could not accept the idea of reincarnation. Now she says: "I have been forced to take it seriously. The amazing physical likenesses, the uncanny things they say, and the similarity in the things they do have made me believe there must be something in it. People have come to the house—people who have not visited since Jacqueline and Joanna died—but the twins recognize them instantly. They always know their names. How *can* you explain away things like this?"

Psychic researchers are asking the same question. "When the children are old enough," says John Pollock, "I shall tell them of my belief that they are really their two sisters returned to earth."

Then they might choose to submit themselves to some sort of hypnosis which might reveal much more about their former lives.

Then, and only then, will new light be shed on the baffling story of the Pollock twins—the girls who, it seems, are living life the second time around. . . .

HAUNTED BY A PHARAOH'S CURSE

After forty years—she still fears vengeance from the tomb . . .

It was as a sightseer that Judith Bickle visited the tomb of Tutankhamen. Ever since, she has been dogged by ill-luck—a victim of the same curse that killed eleven of the first party to enter the tomb years ago.

THE DUST of centuries hung in invisible mouldering folds around the three women. After the relentless sun outside, the tomb was chilled, but by an unnatural coldness.

"Let's go," one of the women said. "I'm frightened." But they did not go. Instead, they moved, unwillingly, as though drawn by invisible hands, further into the dimly-lit shrine of Tutankhamen near Egypt's Valley of the Kings.

Mrs. Judith Bickle and her two friends were merely visitors to the tomb soon after it was discovered by archaeologist Howard Carter after a six-year search in November 1922.

Yet for nearly 40 years the curse of the pharaohs has dogged Mrs. Bickle, her family and her friends.

Nineteen people were in the party which originally broke into the lost tomb. Within ten years, eleven of them were dead. Some died mysteriously, some violently.

Golden graveyard

Mrs. Bickle, guilty only of sightseeing, has been allowed to live. But even today, in her west of England home, she waits in fear for the moment when the dread shadow of the avenging king may again steal over her threshold.

For Mrs. Bickle and her friends the highlight of their Egyptian holiday was to be their visit to the excavations. Tutankhamen's tomb was still largely as Howard Carter had found it.

Nervously, they went down the crumbling stone steps, through the barrier which for 3,265 years had separated the living from the dead, and into a golden graveyard. Among the shadows of dynastic monuments and colossi, bats whirled in an eerie stillness.

They found Tutankhamen in a tiny room, lying under a vast enamel canopy. A lantern hanging in the tomb revealed his tiny, boy-like figure, his face covered with a mask of gold and crystal.

Fled in terror

The women stood, suddenly transfixed with an unknown, illogical dread. Then with a swiftness that caught them completely unprepared, a flurry of movement broke the silence, and one of the women clutched her arm as the teeth of a bat sank into it. Two of the women fled in terror. They rushed blindly through the gloom and out into the comfort of the bright sun.

But Judith Bickle did not follow them. She was gazing with hypnotized fascination at the golden face of the god-king . . . the sacred cobra still coiled on his brow as it had been three thousand years before when the legions of the lost had buried him there.

Forty years later she remembers every plane of that inscrutable, strangely menacing face.

The visit to the tomb is deeply carved on her memory: "There was a cold but musty air about the place and every sound we made echoed and re-echoed. The actual sight of the shrine had a terrible emotional effect on me. My heart and whole body seemed distressed to think we had disturbed the peace of the dead."

But the dead were soon going to demand their own particular kind of retribution.

Mrs. Bickle returned from Cairo and her misfortune began. Within a week both her parents, until then remarkably healthy, became seriously ill. Her mother died. A week later a devoted dog also died. A few days later, Mrs. Bickle's car was stolen. Then followed a break-in at her house and the theft of all her jewelry.

House ablaze

By now she had seriously begun to link up her misfortune with some small relics she had brought back from the tomb. There was logic in her reasoning: the Hon. Richard Bethell, former secretary to Howard Carter died mysteriously in a room littered with Egyptian relics. His father, Lord Westbury, an avid collector of Egyptian antiques jumped to his death from a 70-foot high window.

Mrs. Bickle gathered her souvenirs—some stones from the burial chamber, two scarab beetles, a box containing herbs, and some beads made from pebbles, and threw them into a river.

The effect was magical: for five years her life was smooth and uneventful. Then on the fifth anniversary of the disposal of the relics, things began to go wrong again.

She was involved in a serious car crash. Her father died, and her house caught fire. In the smoldering ruins of her home only one object remained undamaged: a giant picture of Tutankhamen's tomb, in an oil company brochure sent to her husband.

Tormentor destroyed

A few years later, a magazine was delivered to the house. As soon as she touched it, Mrs. Bickle felt a frightened prickling in the scalp. Quickly she leafed through the pages.

There, staring at her with a bland inscrutable gaze was a full-page picture of Tutankhamen. She destroyed her tormentor by fire, but ill-luck was again on the way.

Two relations died unexpectedly; a business venture she was concerned with unaccountably failed. Her health deteriorated. She began to suffer from strange pains which filled her head and body.

Can all these uncanny events really be coincidence? Dr. R. C. Mardrous, a French scholar of ancient Egypt has declared: "I am absolutely certain the Egyptians knew how to condense around their mummies a dynamism by means of a magic ritual."

The ancient Egyptians put it more simply. Above Tutankhamen's head was an inscription which read: "To speak the name of the dead is to make them live again."

THE DREAM THAT CHANGED THE WAR

She spied on Germany's navy . . . in her sleep!

The warning letter from an elderly nurse-maid was regarded as a joke in the Admiralty. At last, someone took heed of her dream—and so stopped the enemy cutting off a vital supplies link which could have changed the course of the war.

As soon as the children were asleep, the old nursemaid sat down and wrote a letter which began: "Dear First Sea Lord, I would like to tell you about my dream . . ."

The letter from Miss Sarah Morris arrived in the department of Lord "Jackie" Fisher, First Sea Lord, in the first week of September, 1914. The typists chuckled over it; senior staff could hardly suppress a smile.

"Do you think," asked Lieutenant-Commander Roger Hamilton, "that we should show it to the Chief? He has precious little to laugh about these days."

The First World War was but a few weeks old and Britain was on the brink of catastrophe on both land and sea. In France, thousands were dying on the Western Front; on water, German U-boats caused havoc in the Grand Fleet.

It seemed hardly the time to bother Lord Fisher with a letter about whales with castles on their backs, nosing around the Forth Bridge . . . so the letter which probably changed the course of the war was tossed into a pending tray until someone found enough initiative to throw it away.

"Something important"

Eventually, Miss Morris's note found its way to the Admiralty's Scottish Command and from there to Commander Michael Gibson, in charge of defences on the Firth of Forth.

Now, for the first time, someone took the letter seriously, which was just as well. If he had not, a vital communications link would have been severed, Britain's Atlantic patrols starved of fuel and ammunition, and the delicate balance of war probably toppled irrevocably in Germany's favor.

Miss Morris had never been to Scotland, but she had seen photographs of the Forth Bridge and recognized it when it appeared in her dream. She saw what she later described as whales with castles on their backs circling around the third pillar of the bridge.

On the following night exactly the same dream occurred again. "I'm sure something important is going to happen," Miss Morris told her employer, Ruth, Countess of Chichester. "I think I should write to the Government."

Vital supplies

"Were they submarines?" someone asked her. "I don't know what they were," replied Miss Morris. "They looked like whales to me. They kept going round and round this pillar."

Commander Gibson was strangely impressed by the letter. At this time of crisis, U-boats were never far from his thoughts. The waters off eastern Scotland were alive with them. The flotilla leader *Pathfinder* had been torpedoed off Thurso, the cruisers *Aboukir, Hogue* and *Cressy* had sunk with a loss of 1,500 men. The destroyer *Hawke* had foundered with 500 men.

These catastrophes had led to an order stopping most day-

light ship movement—which gave U-boats even more free-
dom. But it was inconceivable that submarines would dare
to penetrate the Firth of Forth as far as the mighty bridge.
Or was it . . . ?

Day and night ammunition and supply trains rattled over
the Forth Bridge. Its destruction would cause untold chaos:
the fleets based on Thurso and other Scottish ports would be
starved of vital supplies.

High priority

Why had nothing been done to protect the Forth Bridge?
On his own initiative, Gibson decided to do something
now. He reasoned that the pillars of the bridge would be
safe from submarine attack if they could be cased in concrete to cushion them from shock.

A few days after Miss Morris's letter had arrived in Scotland, construction gangs began to swarm on to the bridge.
The work was given a high priority. Lighters ferried concrete ceaselessly to the bridge. After a week the work was
well advanced.

Intelligence reports gave no indications of submarine activity in the Firth, and Gibson wondered whether his action
was justified.

Work finished

In the first week of October, a patrolling frigate reportated
an unidentified submarine in the sea off the south of the
Firth of Forth.

The same day, Gibson, studying progress sheets of the
Forth Bridge protection plan, noted the work was nearly
complete . . . except for the third pillar. An extra shift was
added and the concreting was finished by the next afternoon.
All known measures to make the bridge safe from submarine
attack had now been taken.

Two days later, on October 7, 1914, the destroyer *Fearless* left Rosyth after boiler repairs, and steamed down the Firth of Forth towards the sea.

She passed under the bridge and was nearly a mile downstream when her lookouts saw two submarines break the surface.

One escaped

Three torpedoes streaked from their tubes towards the third pillar of the bridge. Two missed; the third ricocheted harmlessly from the protective concrete.

Already *Fearless* was firing at the enemy, swinging in a wide arc so that her gunners could aim without fear of hitting the bridge.

One U-boat crash-dived and escaped. The other, a shell buried in her hull, turned over and sank amid plumes of spray.

Miss Morris's dream had come spectacularly to life.

By Charles Fort, the classic

BOOK OF THE DAMNED 50¢ K-156

One of the most startling, unconventional books ever written! Here, too, Charles Fort records the strangest, most astonishing events that have occurred in the world, on which science is strangely silent. The original and greatest compilation of 1,001 attested phenomena that science cannot answer and deliberately ignores. "Charles Fort has made a terrible onslaught upon the accumulated lunacy of fifty centuries. . . . He has shot the scientific basis of modern wisdom full of large, ugly holes."—Ben Hecht

STRANGE WORLD by Frank Edwards 50¢ K-206

All new, all different—the latest collection of astonishing stories taken from life by the author of *Stranger Than Science* and *Strangest of All*. Carefully authenticated, here are 118 incidents, gathered from every corner of the earth—and beyond!—which challenge the logic of layman and scientist alike. "A fascinating book . . ."—*Chicago Tribune*

STRANGER THAN SCIENCE by Frank Edwards 50¢ K-117

One of the most sensational paperback best sellers in America today. A continuing success that has caught the imagination of hundreds of thousands of readers across America. "A fascinating collection of 73 weird, fully-documented stories taken from life that modern science is still powerless to explain . . . Once you have started this book there is no laying it aside until every one of the intriguing, strange stories has been read." —*Colorado Springs Free Press*